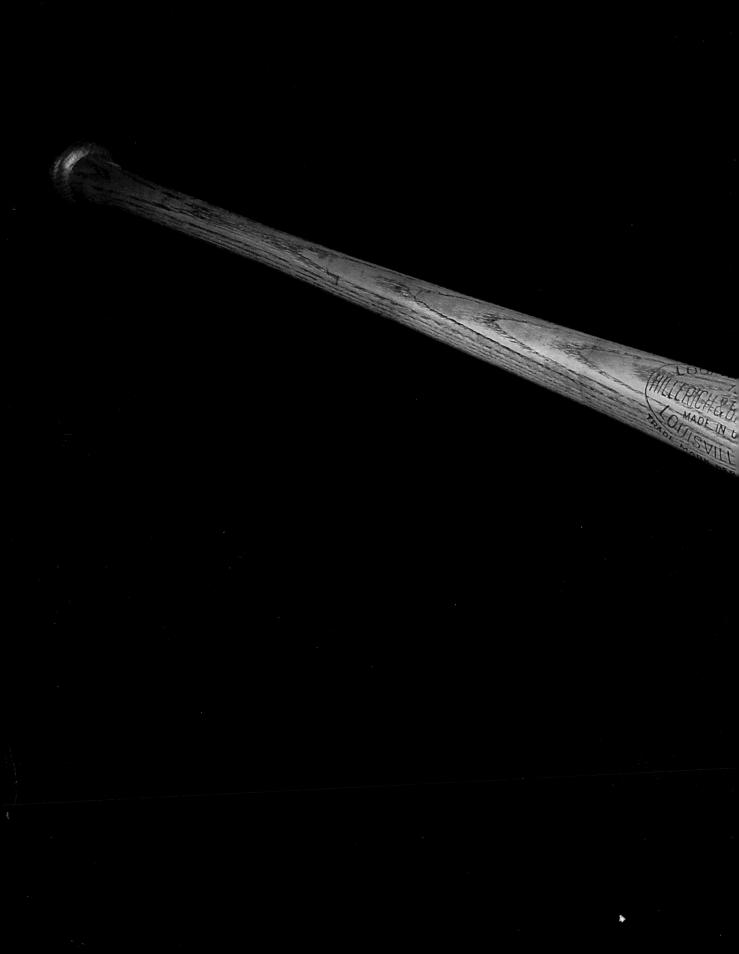

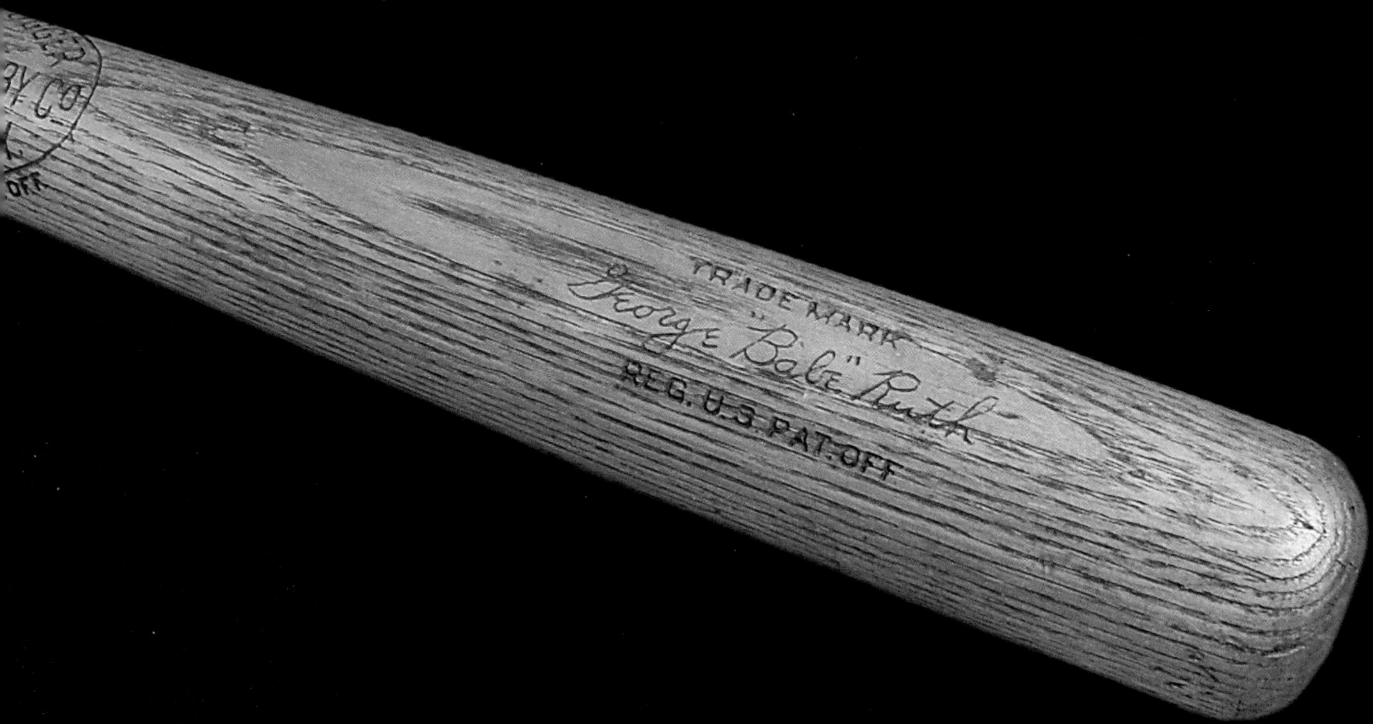
TRADE MARK
George "Babe" Ruth
REG. U.S. PAT. OFF

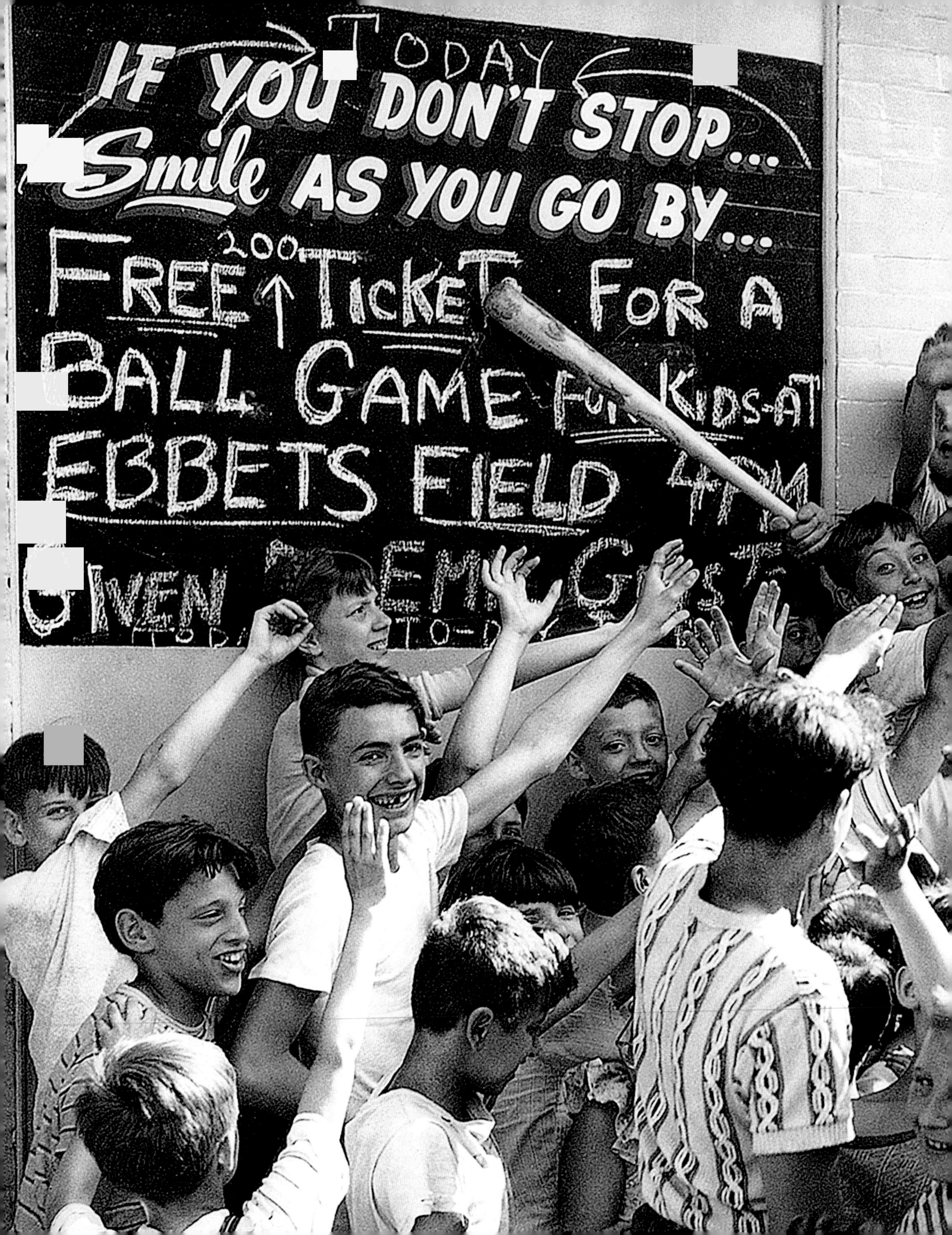
TODAY
IF YOU DON'T STOP...
Smile AS YOU GO BY...
BALL GAME
EBBETS FIELD

Foreword by
Susan Henshaw Jones

Introduction by
Ann Meyerson

Edited by
John Thorn

Under the auspices of
**Museum of the City
of New York**

The Glory Days:
New York Baseball 1947–1957

Collins
An Imprint of HarperCollins*Publishers*

The Glory Days: New York Baseball 1947–57, an exhibition opening in June 2007
President and Director **Susan Henshaw Jones**
Deputy Director and Chief Curator **Sarah M. Henry**
Guest Curator **Ann Meyerson**
Curatorial Consultant **John Thorn**
Exhibition Design **Pentagram**

Museum of the City of New York
1220 Fifth Avenue
New York, New York 10029
212.534-1672
www.mcny.org

Managing Editor **Susan Gail Johnson**
Photography by **David Arky**
Digital Imaging by **Ken Allen Studios**
Design by **Pentagram**
Produced by **Pure+Applied**

ISBN: 978-0-06-134404-6

ISBN-10: 0-06-134404-4

07 08 09 10 11 12 / 10 9 8 7 6 5 4 3 2 1

The Lineup

Foreword

In the early 1950s, New Yorkers walking down many a city street could literally follow the progress of a baseball game through the radios playing in all of the open windows. These were the days before the dominance of television—or air conditioning—but more than that, they were the days when the game of baseball united and divided New Yorkers. New York was baseball crazy. The epic struggles among the Brooklyn Dodgers, the New York Giants, and the New York Yankees symbolized the character of the postwar city.

What more fitting topic for an exhibition at the museum whose mission is to explore New York's identity? No other city had three major league teams—a figurative embodiment of New York's dominance as the largest and most influential city in the country. Each team attracted its distinct group of fans in this diverse urban center, reflecting the complex layering of class, ethnicity, and neighborhood that make up New York's singular character. And, fittingly, New York was where Jackie Robinson broke the color barrier, opening the door not only to African Americans but to Latinos and new immigrants to participate fully in baseball, this most American sport.

The Glory Days: New York Baseball 1947–1957 is published to coincide with an exhibition of the same name at the Museum of the City of New York. This exhibition was the idea of Museum trustee Larry Simon. I thank him for his vision, leadership, and support for this quintessentially New York topic. Leadership funding came from the Homeland Foundation, and I am grateful to E. Lisk Wyckoff for his enthusiasm for baseball history and to the Homeland Foundation for its support. Additional major support was provided by Sandy and Larry Simon, HarperCollins Publishers, James G. Dinan and Elizabeth R. Miller, The Bank of New York, Miller Tabak + Co., Paul E. Singer, a gift in honor of Phil Rizzuto #10 of the New York Yankees—the oldest living Hall of Famer, the James A. Macdonald Foundation, Mr. and Mrs. Newton P.S. Merrill, and Ivy Asset Management Corporation. Other supporters include The Sloan Family Foundation and The Bernard and Toby Nussbaum Foundation. We are delighted to have WPIX TV-CW11 as the official local media partner of *The Glory Days*.

Guest curator Ann Meyerson provided the intellectual backbone and extensive research that went into putting this exhibition together, with the able assistance of curatorial associate Susan Gail Johnson, under the enlightened guidance of the Museum's deputy director and chief curator, Sarah Henry. The subject came to life under the design guidance of Michael Gericke and his team at Pentagram, Inc., which provided the exhibition and graphic design.

Credit for the conception and execution of this book goes to editor John Thorn, who also served as curatorial consultant for the exhibition. We are delighted to be partnering with Collins on this project and are grateful to Phil Friedman and Joe Tessitore for their enthusiasm for the book and the exhibition. Ann Meyerson and Susan Gail Johnson gathered much of the visual historic content for the book, beautifully designed by Pentagram and implemented by Pure+Applied. I am deeply grateful to all who loaned objects and images to the book and to the essayists for their insightful perspectives on what was a joyful and poignant episode in the life of the city.

The exhibition would not have been possible without the guidance of a stellar advisory committee chaired by Larry Simon, Tim Russert, and New York City Sports Commissioner Ken Podziba. I thank them for their leadership and insights, along with committee members Dave Anderson, Marty Appel, Howard Berk, Len Berman, Joe Dorinson, Carl Erskine, Josh Freeman, Harvey Frommer, Lorraine Hamilton, Monte Irvin, Kenneth Jackson, Marvin Korman, Bob Mandt, Ben Matz, Marvin Miller, Ernestine Miller, Tony Morante, Roberta Newman, David Newman, Patricia Paz, Branch B. Rickey, Ray Robinson, Howard Rubenstein, Alan Schwarz, Vin Scully, Jules Tygiel, Deborah Tymon, Stephen Wong, Steve Wulf, and Andrew Zimbalist. The generosity of today's New York teams, the Yankees and the Mets, is a tribute to their pride in their New York City heritage and to the fact that they are creating new glory days every day that they play.

At the Museum of the City of New York, I also thank Eddie Jose Bartolomei, Emerson Beyer, Melanie Bower, Jennifer Juzaitis, Abby Lepold, Barbara Livenstein, Autumn Nyiri, George O'Dell, Julia Van Haaften, Kassy Wilson, Shelley Wilson, and all of the staff for their hard work in bringing the glory days to life.

Susan Henshaw Jones
President and Director,
Museum of the City of New York

Preface

**W**hat was it like, to be alive then? When New York City was the capital of baseball, with three of its five boroughs hosting big-league clubs and the World Series seeming to be municipal property? When the city hosted the greatest game, the greatest pennant race, the greatest teams, greatest center fielders? When everything seemed bigger but somehow personal?

What was it like, to be home from the battle or to welcome a loved one's return? To arrive at the golden door after surviving the ravages of war? To witness the welcome, to the nation and its pastime, of those formerly rebuked and scorned?

What was it like? With this book we wish to tell—but mostly show—you why the era was both glorious and sad and why, for those of us old enough to remember, it seems only yesterday.

The Glory Days is a companion to an exhibition at the Museum of the City of New York that far-flung readers, many of them Gotham alumni, may not be able to visit. The book relies upon the inning structure of the show and the curatorial effort that went into gathering thousands of artifacts, some from the players and playing fields, but also many from the fans whose devotion made the era so memorable. This book forms a "people's hall of fame" for baseball and the city for the years 1947–1957, reflecting Thomas Wolfe's remark that baseball "is part of the whole weather of our lives, of the thing that is our own, of the whole fabric, the million memories of America."

That's it: like a ballpark, this book is a museum of memories. Here "museum quality" does not mean mint condition, to which only dollars attach. In a banged-up, dog-eared baseball card that has rippled in the wind of bicycle spokes, real life resides still. And so it does in our legion of improbable survivors, from a Knothole Gang membership card to a Knickerbocker Beer coaster. The best "collectibles," the keys to revivifying an age, are those that by all rights should have been thrown away and in their survival bear the scars of love.

Among the fabulous survivors we unearthed are glorious color photographs from private archives, never published or not seen in the fifty to sixty years since their only appearance. The museum's LOOK Magazine archives supplied many wonders, while others have come from the treasure trove of SPORT magazine, beloved of all boys back then; the vault of Barney Stein, who photographed the Dodgers so beautifully; and the archive of Hy Peskin, perhaps the greatest of all sports photographers. The pictures tell their thousands of words, from the artifacts waft the aroma of the past, and the writers vividly tell the stories that pictures can't.

The big story of the era in New York, in baseball and in America, was racial integration; Jules Tygiel reminds us in his essay for the first inning that while Jackie Robinson was a hero, he was not the only one. This is a theme that Lee Lowenfish continues with his contrarian "Two Cheers for Horace Stoneham." Perhaps nowhere else but New York could Branch Rickey's great experiment have been launched, and Michael Shapiro reflects in "What Was Lost" upon how important baseball was to the city and vice versa.

There were revolutions in how print and electronic media covered the game and how money was to be extracted from it. George Vecsey warmly recalls the former, while Andrew Zimbalist and Steven Riess incisively detail the latter. For better and sometimes worse, modern baseball was invented in this period. Jonathan Eig's essay on the 1947 World Series, the first fall classic to be televised, rounds out innings 4, 5, and 6.

Kevin Baker's essay for inning 7, "Thomson at the Ferry," takes off from the greatest on-field moment in the history of baseball, the Thomson home run, to look at the city when it too was at its greatest. Jane Leavy answers the question of "Willie, Mickey, or the Duke" with "Forever Mick." Others are entitled to their views, but they are unlikely to write as well.

And then in the era's final year we hit the hard part, except in the Bronx, where the Yankees continued a winning tradition that extends to the present day. Ray Robinson, who saw his first baseball game in 1928, sat in the bleachers for the last game the Giants played in New York, which he recalls in the book's ninth inning, "Farewell to the Polo Grounds." In the book's extra and final inning, Alan Schwarz identifies the real legacy of the era, the one that fills not only Shea and Yankee Stadiums but our hearts as well.

Heretofore when celebrated in print, the glory days of baseball in New York have been tinged in sepia, recalled with syrupy nostalgia. Nostalgia as the Greeks understood that word was not sweet but painful: literally the ache of not being able to return home. Neither New York nor baseball, nor any of us who recall the period, can turn back the clock. Yet we hope this book summons up for you the era the way it really was: colorful, raucous, hopeful, thrilling, crushing. Glorious.

John Thorn
Editor

Introduction

**W**hat better way than through baseball to explore New York City in the first decade after World War II!

As a curator and historian of New York City, this was my thought when the Museum of the City of New York decided to mount an exhibition on the heyday of New York baseball. This was the first time a major museum would treat the subject of the golden era of New York's three teams, when their daring and success combined with a unique time in our nation's history to produce one of the greatest periods in all of American sports. It was a particularly timely moment for this exhibition: 2007 marks the 60th anniversary of Jackie Robinson's breaking the color barrier and the 50th anniversary of the city's two historic National League teams leaving for California.

It's unusual today to find a New Yorker aged 55 or older who does not become animated when one mentions baseball in the 1950s—as if it's never been quite the same since. In many ways, this is true.

Never has there been such a concentration of talented players and managers, spectacular feats and dedicated fans at the same time in one town. From 1947 through 1957, with three major league teams in the city (there were only sixteen in the whole country then) and at least one of them in the World Series every year but one; with two National League rivals squaring off twenty-two times each season; and with seven Subway Series and nine World Series championships, New York City was the undisputed baseball capital of the nation.

But more than that, New Yorkers lived and breathed baseball with an intensity that is hard for us to recapture.

As the exhibition began to take shape, we felt we could not truly explain this phenomenon without looking at factors off the field as well as on. What made this period of baseball in New York unique? Baseball had shaped whole generations of New Yorkers in every decade before World War II, and baseball today is enormously popular as well. So, what was different about this decade?

The era has a particularly powerful hold on fans who grew up in this period for several reasons:

- In the postwar decade, baseball dominated sports culture, and New York City dominated baseball. Unlike today, baseball in effect was the only game in town, not yet fully competing with other league sports such as football or basketball. And its transformation by big business and the television revolution was still to come. The game was concentrated in the northeast, and New York City was the dominant city.

- There was the pride fans felt in being part of the Jackie Robinson story, a history that has a particularly powerful pull for African Americans in New York, but also for Jews whose immigrant parents or grandparents had fled persecution and who had recently lived through the Holocaust, directly or indirectly.

- The era is imbued with an unusually strong dose of nostalgia for one's youth because of the abrupt departure of the Giants and Dodgers in 1957. For the first time in their lives, many young fans suffered a meaningful loss. Even many Yankee fans missed the intensity of all those subway series and friendly arguments.

- Many New Yorkers hunger for the small-town sense of community that baseball had provided in a city on the cusp of being transformed by mass suburbanization. Pent-up consumer demand after the War drove the move to the suburbs, with its more privatized lifestyle and materialistic values—a move that turned out to be a mixed bag for some. Did the folks who fled at the same time as the Dodgers and Giants also leave behind something they never could regain in their lives?

For the readers of this book who will not get a chance to walk through *The Glory Days* at the Museum of the City of New York, what follows is a glimpse of how it plays out, arranged in 10 "innings" or thematic sections.

The opening scene for our story is set by two iconic images from 1947: Babe Ruth in his farewell address to fans, closing one era, and Jackie Robinson entering the Dodgers clubhouse, beginning another. The feeling of the 1950s is enhanced by period music, game sound effects, photomurals of fans at the ballparks, and vintage print advertisements of products associated with the players and their teams—from Jackie Robinson promoting Wheaties, to Bobby Thomson for Bromo Seltzer, to Yogi Berra for Yoo-Hoo chocolate drink, to an unusual vintage subway sign featuring players denouncing racial and religious prejudice.

Because World War II and its immediate aftermath are so critical to our story, the visitor next sees photographs of Jackie Robinson and Joe DiMaggio in military uniform and New Yorkers celebrating V-E Day in Times Square, as well as objects such as war ration stamps and team rosters listing the players serving in the armed forces. Returning players replenished the game as they entered a dramatically changing world. The city's population was also shifting, as mass suburbanization began and newcomers from the South and Puerto Rico arrived.

The exhibition's first "inning," **Breaking the Color Barrier in Brooklyn,** opens with photographs of American segregation: whites-only washrooms in the South and segregated Stuyvesant Town in New York City, along with artifacts from baseball's Negro Leagues. It took a world war and its aftermath to break down America's racially segregated society in the 1940s, of which baseball was an important part. Once African Americans experienced the hypocrisy of fighting for their country at the same time as suffering racial discrimination at home, it wasn't long before desegregation came onto the national agenda. A ticket to Opening Day, April 15, 1947, at Ebbets Field—Jackie Robinson's debut in the major leagues—and a Robinson pennant from his rookie year are two of the iconic objects for this inning. The words of Dodgers president Branch Rickey, who found and signed Robinson, as well as those of Robinson himself and others, are used to get at Rickey's motivations. And black players tell of the enormous obstacles they faced during these pioneering years. But beyond social justice, one of the main points is that, with this formerly untapped pool of talent, the Dodgers stayed at the top of the National League for a decade.

More than anything else, the glory days of New York baseball were about New York **Fans,** the focus of the second inning, who turned to baseball, seeking normalcy and common pleasures after the war. Yes, the baseball was magnificent. But the city's fans, and particularly the distinctive cultures of each team's following, gave the period its special flavor. With three hometown teams, the team you rooted for went a long way toward defining your personal identity. To deviate from the team allegiance of your family or borough put you at some risk.

Visitors can view the kinds of things fans surrounded themselves with in their passion for their teams: everything from game programs and scored scorecards, to Yankees ashtrays, to a Jackie Robinson doll, to pinbacks and ribboned buttons, to player model gloves and spikes, to specially signed balls from the Happy Felton show, to souvenir pennants, to sheet music about the teams, to player board games. A highlight is the famous Sym-phony drum from that beloved Dodgers "orchestra." Voices of fans are brought into the gallery through displayed reminiscences about rooting for their team, about baseball in general, and about what it was like to come of age in this period. All this is placed in context by demographic information about the ethnic and class background of the fans of each of the teams.

Inning Three, **Giants-Dodgers Rivalry,** tells the story of how New York came to have two National League teams and how their competition became, in Leo Durocher's words, "the most intense, heated rivalry in all of sports." In the quintessential event of the rivalry, and what many believe to be the greatest baseball game ever played, Bobby Thomson concluded the third playoff game of 1951 by hitting the "shot heard 'round the world." A surviving phantom 1951 "World Series" press pin, produced by the Dodgers and discarded after the playoff, is an especially poignant artifact on display.

The years 1947–1957 were also a period of change in the media. Radio ushered in the era, while the age of television was in full force at its end. The fourth inning, **Media**, shows visitors the sportswriters, broadcasters, and photographers who delivered baseball to the fans. Back then fans got their baseball news interpreted by the sportswriters and announcers much more than they do today. Local newspapers and newsstand sports magazines abounded. In this inning, visitors also enjoy two multimedia experiences: a pretend-to-be-the-announcer interactive where one can watch a clip of a Yankees game and try to announce the play-by-play, and then compare the result with Mel Allen's; and a "radio" which can play either the Giants announcer Russ Hodges' famous broadcast of Bobby Thomson's home run or the far more subdued call of his Dodgers counterpart, Red Barber.

Nothing brings us back to this period quite as much as the memory of the physical environments where the games were played. Each of the ballparks—Ebbets Field in Brooklyn, the Polo Grounds in Manhattan, and Yankee Stadium in the Bronx—reflected the character of each team and its fans. Yankee Stadium was stately, like the successful team. Ebbets Field was cozy and ramshackle, like the Dodgers. And the Polo Grounds was the grand dame, the oldest extant ballpark with the oldest New York team. Watching the three teams play in the different parks was endlessly fascinating, as one but not another venue might favor left-handed batters or home run sluggers or have a cavernous center field. How each ballpark came to be built and who were the key movers in extracting dollars from them is the subject of the fifth inning, **Ballparks**. On display are seats from all three ballparks, an Ebbets Field usher's uniform and hat, and home plate from the original Yankee Stadium (extensively rebuilt in the 1970s). Visitors to the exhibit are able to transport themselves back to long-demolished Ebbets Field by operating a computer-generated fly-through interactive.

The next three innings—**The World Series; Great Games and Moments;** and **Great Players and Managers**—allow visitors to step directly inside the game and feel the excitement that came with the great concentration of talented players and extraordinary events. Certainly the city is very identified with its teams today—the Yankees and the Mets—and the spirit and intensity of a World Series contest is felt everywhere. But, in the era we celebrate in the exhibition and in this book, the glory days were the World Series, if you were a New Yorker.

In this exhibition, we are very fortunate to bring together, from a variety of private collections, for the first time in one exhibition, game-worn, game-used, and trophy objects to evoke and recapture this golden era: Al Gionfriddo's spikes, worn when he made his implausible 1947 World Series catch; Willie Mays' hat from the 1954 Giants championship season; World Series rings from all three teams; the Dodgers championship banner from 1955; the bat used by Mickey Mantle against the Dodgers in the 1955 World Series; MVP trophies for Yogi Berra and Roy Campanella; a ball used in Don Larsen's 1956 perfect game; game-used gloves and jerseys from such fan favorites as DiMaggio, Irvin, Mantle, and Snider. At the same time, visitors can watch a video of highlights of the great plays narrated by Vin Scully, the legendary Dodgers announcer.

This was the era before the players' union, before free agency, before bidding for players and multimillion-dollar contracts; teams were stable and the players became like family to New Yorkers. The eighth inning, **Great Players and Managers**, focuses on the ball-playing life of the period, when players did not make much money and held down regular jobs out of season. A computer interactive is also included, whereby the visitor can play one of the exhibit's three historic teams against the Mets and the Yankees of the last decade in a tournament to see how well the 1950s teams stack up by today's standards.

The final two sections of the exhibition take us to the ninth inning, **The End**, in 1957, and **Extra Innings: What Came Next**, which provides an epilogue covering 1958 to 2007. Ironically, just as this golden age of baseball was unfolding in New York, the seeds of its decline were beginning to take root. These 11 seasons were the most exciting years in the history of baseball, and yet attendance at games dropped sharply at all three ballparks during the period. Tickets to the last games at Ebbets Field and the Polo Grounds, home plate from the last game at the Polo Grounds, the last Brooklyn flag to fly over Ebbets Field, the demolition signs from both ballparks, and fascinating original documents and telegrams from Walter O'Malley, owner of the Dodgers, and city planner Robert Moses, as well as quotations from Horace Stoneham, owner of the Giants, tell the story of the decision-making that led to the two teams leaving New York within months of each other. But the story here also involves looking at the impact on New Yorkers of the changes taking place in the city's neighborhoods in the 1960s, as suburbanization took off, and block-busting and redlining wreaked havoc.

Although the Dodgers and Giants were in California by 1958, the Yankees continued their dominance of the game through 1964 and then, after some years in the wilderness, they returned to October glory in 1976. Illustrating the transition from the glory days to today are game-worn uniforms and other objects from players on the Dodgers, Giants, and Yankees who joined the Mets when New York's new National League team was born in 1962.

Today New York is a very different city from what it was in 1957, revitalized in part by the greatest immigration in one hundred years. This is reflected in today's multiethnic teams and fans, pioneered by Jackie Robinson and others who opened the door 60 years ago.

It's no wonder that these glory days have had such a hold on New Yorkers, despite the passage of half a century.

Ann Meyerson, Ph.D.
Curator, *The Glory Days*

Batter up!

INNING

1

Breaking Baseball's Color Barrier in Brooklyn

More than Jackie, More than the Dodgers

Jules Tygiel

The image of Jackie Robinson dominates our perceptions of baseball integration. But we often forget that his was just the first act of a lengthy drama that encompassed all three New York teams in the 1940s and 1950s and the rest of the baseball world as well. The introduction of African American players represented an unprecedented social experiment, with the New York franchises becoming laboratories of racial change—each in its own distinctive way.

The Brooklyn Dodgers, of course, led the way. For the 1946 season they had signed not only Robinson, but also catcher Roy Campanella, pitcher Don Newcombe, and others to play in their minor league system. Robinson joined the parent club in 1947, followed by Dan Bankhead, who in August became the first black pitcher in the majors. From 1949 through 1956 Robinson, Campanella, and Newcombe would form a nucleus for the great Dodger teams of the era.

Nonetheless, the Dodgers did not fully pursue their opportunities in recruiting Negro League stars. Their 1945–46

Facing page:
Jackie Robinson wrote the story of the era, July 1949.
Museum of the City of New York, LOOK Collection, photograph by Frank Bauman

> **Baseball has done more to move America in the right direction than all the professional patriots with their billions of cheap words.**
> MONTE IRVIN

**Jackie Robinson and
Branch Rickey, 1947**
Courtesy of the National
Baseball Hall
of Fame Library,
Cooperstown, N.Y.

When we moved
from Bed-Stuy to
Carroll Street in
Crown Heights, we
were one of the first
black families in
that neighborhood.
Everybody was very
civil. But when we
were bused into
Winthrop Junior High,
we made sure not to
wear our better clothes
on Fridays, because
we knew we would
have to fight our way
home. The white kids
from Pigtown would
waylay us.

ROGER GREEN,

*It Happened
In Brooklyn,* 1993

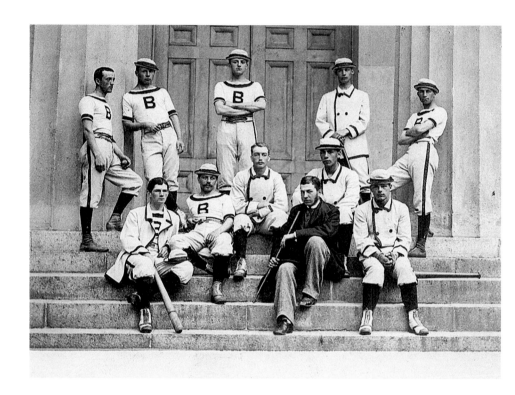

**The first African
American in the
major leagues:
William Edward
White, here shown
with 1879 Brown
U. team, seated
second from left**
Courtesy of John R. Husman

scouting gave them a decided head start over other teams who lacked even a modicum of perception of the riches awaiting them in black baseball. In addition, the Dodgers held a great appeal among African American players, many of whom wanted to play for the team that had signed Jackie Robinson. In the late 1940s and early 1950s the Dodgers plumbed the Negro Leagues to sign standouts like Sam Jethroe, Jim Pendelton, Joe Black, and Jim Gilliam; but Dodger President Branch Rickey passed on other, even better players in order to further the spread of integration.

Larry Doby, universally regarded by major league scouts as the best young prospect in the Negro Leagues, wanted to sign with the Dodgers. However, when the Cleveland Indians expressed an interest, Rickey instructed, "By all means, let him go over to the other league. It will help the movement." The Dodgers reached a personal agreement with Monte Irvin, perhaps the greatest of the postwar Negro League stars, but when the Newark Eagles sold Irvin's contract to the New York Giants, Rickey did not object. "He wanted Negro ballplayers on other clubs," explained an aide.

The Giants had moved hesitantly into the new era. The Dodgers had announced Robinson's signing in 1945. But even after his extraordinary successes at Montreal in 1946 and Brooklyn in 1947, the squires of the Polo Grounds had made no effort to bring in black players. The New York club finally made the leap in 1949, signing Irvin, infielder Hank Thompson, and pitcher Ford Smith to play for their Jersey City franchise. After Irvin pounded Triple-A pitching at a .373 clip for three months, the Giants promoted him and Thompson to the parent club in July. Their efforts beyond this appear relatively modest. Nonetheless, in June 1950, they made the most significant acquisition from the Negro Leagues since Robinson. The Giants signed Willie Mays, the 19-year-old center fielder of the Birmingham Black Barons. Less than a year later he made his major league debut. In 1951 the Dodgers and Giants accounted for all but one of the African American players in the National League.

From the vantage point of 1949, the failure of the Yankees to follow the Dodgers and Giants along the path to integration did not seem a foregone conclusion. Dan Topping, who owned the American League club, had already signed black All-American Buddy Young to play for his football Yankees. General manager Larry MacPhail, who had repeatedly attempted to blunt and criticize efforts to bring African American players to the majors, had left the team after the 1947 World Series. The new management seemed less reluctant to consider Negro League stars and had several advantages in this pursuit. The Yankees rented their facilities in Kansas City and Newark to the Monarchs and the Eagles, respectively, and had close relationships with the owners of those teams. Effa Manley of the Eagles offered her two top stars, Monte Irvin and Larry Doby, to the Yankees before selling them to the Giants and Cleveland Indians. Monarchs co-owner Tom Baird wrote to the Yankees in January 1949, "I feel as though I am a part of the Yankee organization and I want to give you first chance at any players that your organization might want."

Hank Greenberg, early enlistee in WWII and Robinson ally, c. 1944
Private collection

Branch Rickey, c. 1950
Private collection

Subway poster fighting racism; players of different faiths, race, ethnicity (Institute for American Democracy, 1949)
From the collection of Jerry Stern, photograph by David Arky

Baseball Commissioner "Happy" Chandler
Private collection

All American Girls Baseball League, Peoria Red Wings and Grand Rapids Chicks uniform patches, c. 1946

The Bruce Dorskind Collection, photograph by David Arky

N.Y. Black Yankees pinback, c. 1947

The Bruce Dorskind Collection, photograph by David Arky

Pennant for Jackie Robinson's All-Stars, a barnstorming team of 1953-54

From the collection of Jerry Stern, photograph by David Arky

Black Yankees pennant

The Bruce Dorskind Collection, photograph by David Arky

During the course of the 1949 season the Yankees signed five Negro League stars to play for the Newark Bears, their top farm club, prompting Dan Daniel to comment, "Our three local baseball clubs are engaged in a carnival of acquisition of Negro players." The players included Artie Wilson, Luis Angel Marquez, and Bob Thurman, all of whom would eventually reach the major leagues. Thurman had a fine season at Newark, batting .317 and launching several tape-measure home runs. All of the players, however, were gone from the Yankee organization at the start of the 1950 season.

In 1950 the Yankees abandoned the practice of signing established Negro League stars and turned instead to younger players. From Kansas City they signed 21-year-old catcher/outfielder Elston Howard and 24-year-old pitcher Frank Barnes. They turned to the Provincial League in Canada where they discovered two Puerto Rican players, 22-year-old outfielder Vic Power and 21-year-old pitcher Ruben Gomez. The Yankees quickly traded Barnes, who became a longtime minor league standout, and released Gomez, who later starred for the Giants. Howard and Power were left to compete to become the first black Yankee. With these signings the club retreated. Other than Howard and Power, no other African American or Latino player would rise through the Yankee system until the 1960s.

The Yankees were not alone in their reluctance to field non-whites. As late as September 1953, only six of the sixteen major league clubs had broken the color barrier. But the Yankees' failure, juxtaposed against the examples of the Dodgers and Giants, opened the third New York club to considerable criticism. The controversy flared in 1952 when Jackie Robinson, responding to a question on the television show "Youth Wants to Know," asserted: "I think the Yankee management is prejudiced. There isn't a single Negro on the team now and very few in the entire Yankee farm system." The Yankee denials lacked credibility. "We've been looking for a Negro player for years," responded general manager George Weiss. He challenged Robinson to "get me a free agent who is capable of taking the job of any Yankee regular." Weiss thus argued, remarkably, that it was Robinson's responsibility to uncover black athletes for the Yankees and that a black substitute would not merit consideration.

Weiss's reaction reinforced the general image of the racial attitudes that permeated the Yankee organization. A club executive told sportswriter Roger Kahn that, "It would offend boxholders from Westchester to have to sit with niggers." The traveling secretary avowed, "No nigger will ever have a berth on any train I am running."

Manager Casey Stengel referred to black ballplayers as jigs, jigaboos, and jungle bunnies. After Robinson struck out three times against Native American pitcher Allie

There was no consciousness of discrimination in my realm of thought when I joined the Eagles. I was a Negro in Negro baseball. Negroes were barred from organized ball and it looked as if the ban would never be lifted. In fact, I was so little interested in white ball that I did not see a big-league game until 1946, when I saw the Yanks and Dodgers play at Yankee Stadium. DON NEWCOMBE

The great Josh Gibson, c. 1935
Private collection

Reynolds in the 1952 World Series, Stengel commented, "Before that black son-of-a-bitch accuses us of being prejudiced, he should learn how to hit an Indian."

The Yankees fanned the flames in 1953 when they failed to promote Vic Power, who had excelled in the top-level American Association, and then traded him to the Philadelphia Athletics. They circulated reports that Power was "a poor fielder," "not too quick on the trigger mentally," "hard to handle," and lacked the "right attitude" to be a Yankee. Power's subsequent major league career belied these accusations. The Yankees compounded matters by returning Howard to the minors after spring training in 1954, prolonging the team's Jim Crow era. Howard finally made the club in 1955.

The reality of fielding an integrated baseball team posed numerous problems for the three New York clubs. Given the magnitude of the social experiment involved, the path proved generally smooth, but bumps nonetheless appeared on the road. An informal quota system, inspired by a fear of fielding too many non-whites, appeared on all three squads. For the Yankees the quota until 1955 was clearly zero, but both the Dodgers and Giants wrestled with the problem of how many black players might be too many. In 1950 Branch Rickey sold outfield standout Sam Jethroe to the Boston Braves, explaining, "Ownership thought there was a surfeit of colored boys on the Brooklyn club…. [If] a fifth one would tend to lose a pennant, then the reason for hiring Robinson was the identical reason for not hiring Jethroe." In 1951 the Giants opened the season with four African Americans—Irvin, Thompson, catcher Ray Noble, and shortstop Artie Wilson. They kept future Hall of Fame third baseman Ray Dandridge, the 1950 American Association Most Valuable Player, on their Minnesota farm team for the third consecutive year. When Willie Mays unexpectedly proved himself ready for the majors in May, they cut Wilson to make room for him. An injury to third baseman Thompson in July seemed to finally open a spot for Dandridge. But the veteran had just had his appendix removed, forcing the Giants, in a fateful move, to plug Bobby Thomson into the open position.

White players voiced discontent as more African Americans threatened to take up their roster slots. The Giants raised eyebrows in the 1951 World Series when they

Jackie Robinson with barnstorming Kansas City Royals; in San Diego, October 1945 Courtesy of the National Baseball Hall of Fame Library, Cooperstown, N.Y., photograph by Maurice Terrell

Clyde Sukeforth managed Jackie Robinson in his major league debut.
From the collection of Angela and Thomas Sarro

Jackie Robinson comic book, by Charles O. Dexter, Fawcett 1952 Courtesy of Brian Strum, photograph by David Arky

1945 Dodger roster showing players in service From the collection of Jerry Stern

"Time to score for civil rights; give—join NAACP" large poster, 1958 The Bruce Dorskind Collection, photograph by David Arky

As the 1949 song "Did You See Jackie Robinson Hit That Ball" has it, Jackie's real gone. Private collection

started an all-black outfield of Irvin, Mays, and Thompson. After the Dodgers made Jim Gilliam their starting second baseman in 1953, a teammate complained: "I don't mind them in the game, but now they're really taking over." Similar rumblings were heard the next year when Sandy Amoros joined the squad. Speculation now surfaced about whether or not a team might feature a lineup in which blacks outnumbered whites. The Dodgers could have Newcombe or Joe Black pitching with Robinson, Campanella, Gilliam, and Amoros in the field. For the first three months of the 1954 season the Dodgers never played more than four of their black players at the same time. Not until July 17 did they break the barrier.

Nor did racial sensitivities predominate in the locker rooms. According to one account, Giants manager Leo Durocher told his black players, "If the game gets close and tense, I may be shouting 'nigger' and 'watermelon' at guys on the other side like Jackie Robinson. But I want you guys to understand that you are on my team." Casey Stengel called Elston Howard "Eightball," and after seeing him play famously commented, "When I finally get a nigger, I get the only one that can't run." Alabaman Eddie Stanky nicknamed his Giants teammate Ray Noble, "Bushman." With teammate Monte Irvin standing next to him, Stanky shouted at Robinson, "Stick that bat down your throat, you black nigger son of a bitch."

Facing page: **Jackie Robinson working out with the Kansas City Royals, in San Diego, October 1945** Courtesy of the National Baseball Hall of Fame Library, Cooperstown, N.Y., photograph by Maurice Terrell

The one thing that concerned Jack was the possibility of an overenthusiastic black response. We saw it more in the South than in Brooklyn, but every time he came up to bat early on, even if he hit a pop-up, there would be a tremendous reaction. We worried this overresponse would lead to fights in the ballpark, but it didn't happen.

RACHEL ROBINSON,
It Happened in Brooklyn,
1993

Jackie Robinson, 1948
Leaf card Courtesy of
Kevin Bean

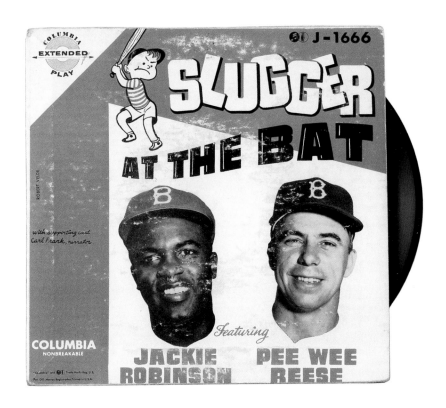

"Slugger at the Bat," c. 1949
Courtesy of Brian Strum, photograph by David Arky

Roy Campanella, 1956
Topps card Courtesy of
Kevin Bean

When Robinson retired in 1956 the racial profiles of the three teams had become fixed, although not necessarily in the manner one would have expected. The recruitment of non-white players had changed dramatically. In the early years the hunt for African American and Latino talent usually meant scouting the Negro Leagues. With the rapid collapse of those teams, major league clubs had to scout black sandlots, high schools, and colleges and extend operations into the Caribbean. The Yankees, predictably, lagged behind in these endeavors. After promoting Howard in 1955, they added Harry "Suitcase" Simpson via a trade for the 1957 and 1958 seasons, but did not produce another African American player through their farm system until 1963, when Al Downing, who had made token appearances in 1961 and 1962, joined the pitching rotation. Nor did the Yankees develop any Latino players, though they did acquire Panamanian Hector Lopez and Puerto Rican Luis Arroyo in trades in 1959 and 1960.

Surprisingly the Dodgers had not fared that much better. They still profited from the bounty of standouts they had procured from the Negro Leagues. They also made a small dent in the Caribbean market. Cuban Sandy Amoros joined the team in 1954 and remained through the Brooklyn years. The Dodgers signed but then lost Roberto Clemente before he had ever donned a Brooklyn uniform. Two other Cuban players, Chico Fernandez and Rene "the Whip" Valdez, had short-lived stays in Brooklyn. In 1957, their last year in Brooklyn, the non-white contingent on the Dodgers included the clearly aging Campanella and Newcombe, the steadfast Gilliam, Amoros, infielder Charlie Neal, and, after midseason, catcher John Roseboro, the first African American on the Dodgers with no connection to the Negro Leagues. Beyond those players the cupboard was almost bare. The minor leagues featured only one African American prospect, Tommy Davis, who would go on to play for the Dodgers. Remarkably, after Newcombe was traded during the team's first season in Los Angeles, no other African American or Caribbean-born pitcher would take the mound for the Dodgers until Jim "Mudcat" Grant in 1968. Nor did the Dodgers produce any Latino stars during this era.

The situation was quite different in the Giants organization. During the Negro League era, the Giants had rented the Polo Grounds to the New York Cubans. When that club collapsed, the Giants employed Cubans owner Alex Pompez to scout the Caribbean for talent. Pompez, who once ran a lucrative illegal gambling operation as one of the numbers kings of Harlem, had a long history in baseball dating back to the 1910s. He had introduced many of the top Cuban players to the United States and had extensive connections throughout the Caribbean. He also had an extraordinary eye for talent. In 1953 he brought in Puerto Rican Ruben Gomez, discarded by the Yankees, to pitch for the Giants. In 1954 he added Venezuelan Ramon Monzant. In 1956, catcher Ozzie Virgil became the first native of the Dominican Republic to play in the majors. The 1957 Giants featured players from the Dominican Republic, Puerto Rico, the Bahamas, and Cuba, to complement Mays. Pompez also played a major role in discovering and signing young African American players.

Thus, when the Giants left New York in 1957 they had an extraordinary pool of non-white talent under contract in the minor leagues. The assemblage included African Americans Bill White (who had been the everyday first baseman with the Giants in 1956), Leon Wagner, Willie McCovey, and Willie Kirkland; Puerto Rican sensation Orlando Cepeda and his countryman Jose Pagan; and Dominicans Felipe and Mateo Alou and Juan Marichal. All except White, who would become an All Star with the Cardinals, would go on to shine for the Giants. McCovey, Cepeda, and Marichal would join Mays in the Hall of Fame. The Brooklyn Dodgers had engineered baseball's historic racial breakthrough, but the Giants—even before they departed for San Francisco—had pioneered the modern multicultural, international game that integration had made possible.

Elston Howard, in 1955 the first African American to play for the Yankees Private collection

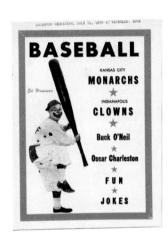

The Negro Leagues on their deathbed; 1954 Kansas City Monarchs program
Library of Congress

Orlando Cepeda never played in New York, but he was a Robinson legacy. Private collection

Roy Campanella with the Baltimore Elite Giants, 1944-45 Private collection

Wilson Official Negro American League baseball in box, c. 1950 The Bruce Dorskind Collection, photograph by David Arky

Facing page:
Satchel Paige, a 42-year-old major-league "rookie" in 1948
Private collection

INNING

Fans
What Was Lost
Michael Shapiro

I grew up in a Brooklyn that had no Dodgers and came of age believing that had the team not left, life would have been different and better.

I just missed them. I was born in 1952 and by the time I was aware of the world and of baseball, the Dodgers were gone. I never went to Ebbets Field, although I can recall, hazily, once seeing the team on television. I do remember the day in 1960 Ebbets Field was torn down, because the older boys down the block showed me the bricks and dirt they carried home.

I grew up believing that I had missed something grand, although I could not explain precisely what it was. For the longest time I felt a bit foolish about this sense of loss for what I never had. It was, after all, one thing to have followed the Dodgers, and better still to stake those claims to a connection that was uniquely Brooklyn: "we used the same pediatrician as Pee Wee Reese;" "Jackie Robinson was at my Bar Mitzvah;" "my uncle was Duke Snider's ophthalmologist. Really."

I, on the other hand, once saw Gil Hodges outside Midwood Field on Avenue K. But he was then the manager of the Mets, so that didn't count.

Dodgerless Brooklyn was not necessarily a bad place—although by the time I became a teenager it was understood that there were subway stops where it was not safe to change trains. But it wasn't much of anything. Brooklyn, of course, has now become a very cool place, and I am still taken aback when my teenage daughter tells me that she is going shopping at boutiques in Williamsburg with friends from Park Slope. Suffice it to say that my father grew up in a Williamsburg where people shopped primarily for groceries and dry goods. The transformation isn't surprising: Brooklyn has historically been a place that reinvented itself; people came and rented for a while before moving

Facing page:
Fans typically exited onto the field, here after Don Larsen's perfect game, 1956.
Museum of the City of New York, LOOK Collection, photograph by Arnold Newman

Sal Maglie pitched for all three New York teams; in this 1952 Bowman card he is a Giant.
Courtesy of Kevin Bean

Whitey Ford, 1951 Bowman card
Courtesy of Kevin Bean

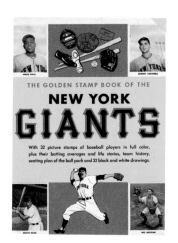

Golden Stamp Book, 1955

Courtesy of Jerry Liebowitz

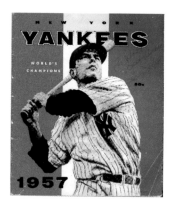

Yankees Yearbook, 1957

Courtesy of Jerry Birnbach

on to someplace else—livelier maybe, or with newer homes and bigger yards. It was not necessarily a place to stay, if only because there wasn't much to keep you, especially after the Dodgers moved away.

I left when I was 21, but I still carried with me a gnawing sense that I wished I had been a little older, so that I might have felt what I was sure I had missed. Later, I learned that this vague feeling of loss was not mine alone. I began hearing much the same lament from friends with whom I grew up. Still, it was not until professional baseball returned to Brooklyn in 2001 with the minor league Cyclones that I understood how pervasive this sentiment was. In the buildup to the team's Coney Island debut, the Cyclones' website invited prospective fans to post their feelings about the coming of the team.

There were the expected encomiums from those who remembered the Dodgers, sepia-tinged memories that suggested a Brooklyn where the sun always shone on Ebbets Field. But the surprising comments came from men and women who, like me, had grown up hearing about what it had been like, a long time ago—stories told and retold and which always ended with the same, dark conclusion: When that bastard O'Malley took the Dodgers out of Brooklyn, he tore the heart out of the borough.

Or similar depictions of Dante-like anguish.

Brooklyn's pain for its loss has endured well into its second generation, a phenomenon that defies logic. After all, St. Louis suffered the defection of the Browns. The Athletics left Philadelphia and Kansas City, too, just as the Braves abandoned Boston and then Milwaukee. The Giants left Manhattan, within days of the Dodgers' departure. And while I know of people who cannot hear the words "Coogan's Bluff" without getting misty, I am reasonably confident that the loss does not carry the enduring sting of the disappearance of Brooklyn's Dodgers.

The Brooklyn Dodgers, I submit, represent the epitome of baseball loss. Consider the circumstances: They were a very bad team for much of their history; then in 1941, they started getting good; between 1947 and 1957 they were the best team in the National League and the second best team in baseball, surpassed only by the Yankees, except in 1955, when for the one and only time they won it all; then, three years later, before love could turn to ruin, they vanished. Remember, too, that while the Dodgers had begun play way back when Brooklyn was a city unto itself, in the twentieth century they were not a city's team. They were the team of a part of a city, a borough, a legal entity that in no way can begin to capture the feeling of second-best-ness that for so many decades afflicted Brooklyn, especially in comparison to the thin, rich, and glittery island on the far side of the East River. The Dodgers lived in Brooklyn. Kids

Facing page:

What was a rooter without regalia? October 7, 1953

Courtesy of the Brooklyn Public Library–Brooklyn Collection

Green Bros. and Knight Music Publishers, 1943

The Bruce Dorskind Collection, photograph by David Arky

Dixie Cup lid with Preacher Roe... and ancient ice cream

Courtesy of Brian Strum

Baseball entered the home not only via the media. Courtesy of Brian Strum, photograph by David Arky

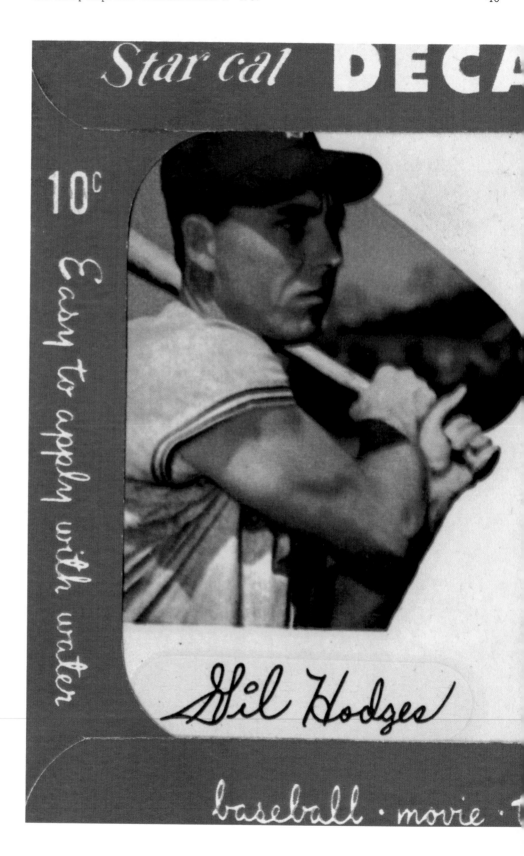

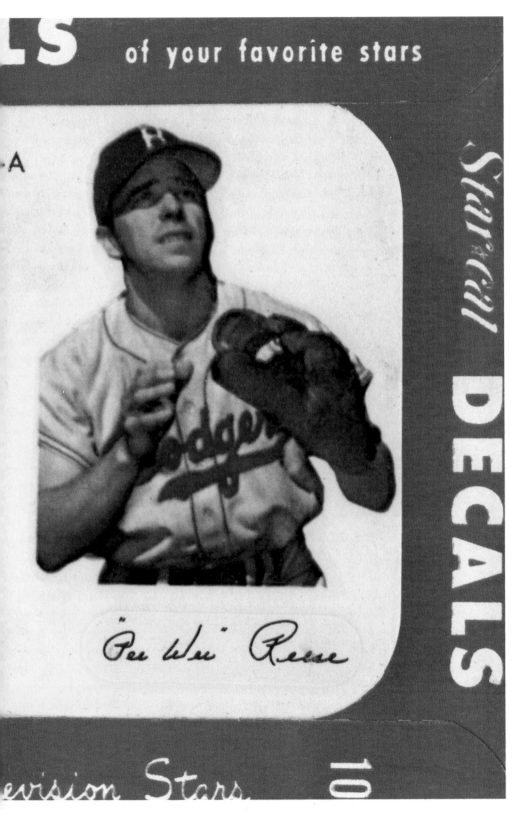

of your favorite stars

Starcal DECALS

-A

"Pee Wee" Reese

evision Stars. 10

Many of us were first-generation Americans, and we were given strong doses of patriotic indoctrination. Assemblies began with a color guard processional, with a huge American flag. We were dressed all alike: girls in white middy blouses with red ties and navy pleated skirts, boys in white shirts, red ties, and navy pants. We sang a lot of hymns and all the Christmas carols, even though at least half of the children were Jewish. But no one seemed to mind.

MARNIE BERNSTEIN,
It Happened in Brooklyn, 1993

Left:
Reese and Hodges decals—"easy to apply with water;" sure. Courtesy of Brian Strum

1949 "HoJo the Bum" squeaky doll, by Rempel Manufacturing of Akron, OH Courtesy of Brian Strum, photograph by David Arky

Top:
Up close and personal with Eddie Lopat, June 1954 Museum of the City of New York, LOOK Collection, photography by Robert Lerner and Arthur Rothstein

Facing page:
Jackie Robinson with beaming acolyte, 1951 Private collection

My brother Gary came back from visiting a friend who had moved out to Long Island. "It's terrible there," he said. "They have to sleep in their own room."
STAN GOLDBERG,
It Happened in Brooklyn, 1993

rang Pee Wee's doorbell for autographs. I never met anyone who rang Mickey Mantle's doorbell, looking for an autograph.

Now, it is important to remember that the Dodgers' departure was hardly like the escape under cover of darkness engineered by Robert Irsay when he took his Colts from Baltimore to Indianapolis. People knew the Dodgers were leaving. They had heard about the possibility for so many months that when the news finally came that the team was leaving, the men and women who loved the Dodgers did not take to the streets, tear at their garments and don sackcloth and ash. In fact, the reaction was—hard as it is to believe now—rather muted. Weary of the back-and-forth between Brooklyn and Los Angeles, people sounded as if they were, if anything, beyond caring.

So here we are, fifty years later, and the Seattle-based purveyor of newly fabricated oldtime jerseys and caps calls itself Ebbets Field Flannels. Was this merely a bow to a ballpark that no longer stands? Or was it a clever use of a name that, more than any other, is a metaphor for a long-ago and longed-for time—an era that every vintage ballpark and $375 replica jersey tries to recapture?

I have been feeling the tug all my life. I have sat in Camden Yards. I own six Brooklyn Dodger baseball caps. None of these brought me closer to understanding what I was sure I lost with the Dodgers' departure.

And then, I found it. Not in Brooklyn. Not even in New York. But in a faraway place where I made the mistake of thinking that baseball, and what we need from it, is universal.

I went to many baseball games in Japan. I lived there for almost five years and went to games in Tokyo, Osaka, and Kawasaki. I spoke

"Put it Here Mickey!" October, 1956
Museum of the City of New York, LOOK Collection, photograph by Arnold Newman

Today's generation of fans could really use this book. Courtesy of Brian Strum

In the offseason players had real jobs; here, Phil Rizzuto as haberdasher, February 1951.
Museum of the City of New York, LOOK Collection, photograph by Frank Bauman

We came from Eastover, a little town in South Carolina. My father only went to third grade. Like everybody else, he farmed. They heard there were better jobs up in New York. That was 1945. Our mother, who had a college education, had to work as a maid. Still, Harlem was such a nice community when I was growing up. The supers used to hose down the sidewalk every morning. We had PAL teams. A lady on our block organized games, had a basketball hoop put up. ALVIN REED, *It Happened in Manhattan, 2001*

enough Japanese to get by, which meant that I could chat a little about unimportant things. There is much made of how baseball in Japan differs from baseball in the United States both in the style of play—historically, a risk-averse approach in a risk-averse culture—and in the stands, where cheering is a group activity (there are cheerleaders with megaphones and flags) and where booing, at least in my time, was not done.

But I did not truly understand the depth of the difference until the night I found myself at Aoyama Stadium, in central Tokyo, watching the Yakult Swallows. I was sitting in the grandstand next to a man in a suit. Something exceptional happened on the field; I don't recall what precisely. I remember only that it was a play worthy of comment. I turned to the man at my side and said, in passable Japanese, something along the lines of "Nice play, huh?"

He looked at me. And then he looked away. He said nothing. I suspect he may have checked my lapel for a company pin. But then I wasn't wearing a jacket. I had not introduced myself, presenting a name card which he could examine, the better to determine my status and therefore his conversational approach. I was, in a word, a stranger. Which meant that he was under no obligation to speak with me. And he didn't.

I did not appreciate this moment in all its cultural wonder until I was back in New York a few weeks later. I was at Shea, with my brother. The Mets were playing the Cardinals and were winning big. We sat in the upper deck, surrounded by strangers. It did not take long before we started chatting. From the chatting came offers to buy beer if we'd watch their kids when they went to the john. And so on. And so on. I had done much the same thing at every ballgame I'd ever attended, having paid no mind to it until I came back from Japan.

I loved it. I loved the banal chatter. I loved the high fives. And I loved the fact that at the end of the game no one said, God forbid, "Say, I really enjoyed talking with you. We should be friends."

Instead, we said what Americans always say to the strangers with whom they have shared a game. We said, "Bye."

We do not follow baseball for the game alone. We follow the game for the conversation. And there is no conversation quite like the one we share about baseball.

Unlike any other sport, there is a game most every day for half the year, not including spring training. And when it rains or there is an off-day, there is always the anticipation of another game just beyond the horizon. This means that talk can shift from past to present to future, barely missing a beat. Each game, of course, offers moments to be chewed over; but it offers numbers, too—statistics to be factored in with the many numbers already filed in the memory bank.

Above:

The mention of Happy Felton's Knothole Gang invariably brings a smile, May 1951.

Museum of the City of New York, LOOK Collection

Bottom left:

The fearsome Hilda Chester and her cowbell

Courtesy of the National Baseball Hall of Fame Library, Cooperstown, N.Y.

Below:

Exuberance and Ebbets were like peanut butter and jelly, October 1, 1950.

Courtesy of the Brooklyn Public Library–Brooklyn Collection

Above:
**The Honeymooners'
Ed Norton in the flesh**

Courtesy of the National Baseball Hall
of Fame Library, Cooperstown, N.Y.

Below:
**Dodger Sym-Phony Band:
savage breasts not soothed here.**

Courtesy of the National Baseball Hall of Fame
Library, Cooperstown, N.Y.

INSIDE BASEBALL
FOR LITTLE LEAGUERS

HINTS ON HOW TO PLAY BETTER BASEBALL

2516

**Step-by-step Picture-Coaching
By Top Stars of the Diamond —**

JACKIE ROBINSON	EDDIE MATHEWS
ROBIN ROBERTS	TED WILLIAMS
CHICO CARRESQUEL	AL ROSEN
STAN MUSIAL	YOGI BERRA

. . . And 20 Other Big League Stars

WONDER BOOKS

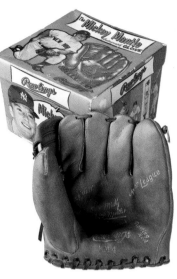

The conversation does not begin with Opening Day. It begins when the season ends and the speculation and lamentation of what might have been begins. It lasts through the fall and into winter through the first sighting in the sports pages of the words, "pitchers and catchers report." Baseball talk started over a hundred years ago and has never stopped.

Except in Brooklyn.

Granted, it was possible in post-Dodger Brooklyn to talk about the Yankees (I did; I'm sorry but I had no one else when I became a fan in 1961) and then about the Mets. But these were New York teams, which meant that the talk was akin to gossiping about someone else's relatives. Interesting, to be sure. But lacking in emotional umph.

The beauty of baseball talk is that it can take place in the ballpark or anyplace else where strangers run into each other. Jane Jacobs, the great celebrator of the American city, believed that the glory of cities was to be found not in grand buildings, but in neighborhood life, in the everyday chitchat that allowed strangers to feel connected to one another. Jacobs would wander down sidewalks in less-than-fashionable neighborhoods and see not buildings destined for the wrecking ball (as did her chief detractor, Robert Moses, the man who built modern New York) but the people who sat on the stoops and chatted at the butcher shop and hung out on the corner. She saw a world that faced out toward the street—toward other people—rather than toward the pleasant suburban view of a backyard of one's own.

The talk was not limited to baseball, or even to sports. But sports talk endured, generation after generation, primarily because each game meant an event that only appeared to matter. No one's life really changed because a team won or lost. Yet that moment when the outcome is in doubt, when happiness and despair hang in the balance, really does approximate the sensation of waiting to learn news of consequence. It is difficult to imagine a life without the surrogate anxieties that baseball so generously provides.

The Rawlings Mickey Mantle MM4 model glove: every boy's dream present. Courtesy of Bob and Adelyn Mayer, photograph by David Arky

Dodgers visor: throwaway trinket then, treasure today. From the collection of Jerry Stern

Visor branded by Tip-Top Bread, former backer of the Brooklyn Federal League entry. Courtesy of Brian Strum

Facing page:
Duke Snider's unorthodox swing was no model for kids. Private collection

Right:
Glide across center field in your Joe DiMaggio baseball cleats, Endicott Johnson, c. 1950. Courtesy of Bob and Adelyn Mayer, photograph by David Arky

HoJo the Bum, with plush dolls so ugly they're beautiful.
Courtesy of Brian Strum, photograph by David Arky

Beer, tobacco and "The Sporting News" spelled baseball in 1956, when this guide was issued.
From the collection of Angela and Thomas Sarro, photograph by David Arky

A Golden Stamp Book was issued for the Dodgers and Giants in 1955 but not the Yankees.
Courtesy of Brian Strum, photograph by David Arky

**Yankee fan Bill
Horowitz, the view
from his apartment
window, and his
taped stick-ball**
Courtesy of Bill Horowitz,
photograph by David Arky

**Mickey Mantle
board game**
Courtesy of Gary Cypres,
photograph by Susan
Einstein, Los Angeles

**Yankee program
and souvenir
coasters** Courtesy of
Bob and Adelyn Mayer,
photograph by David Arky

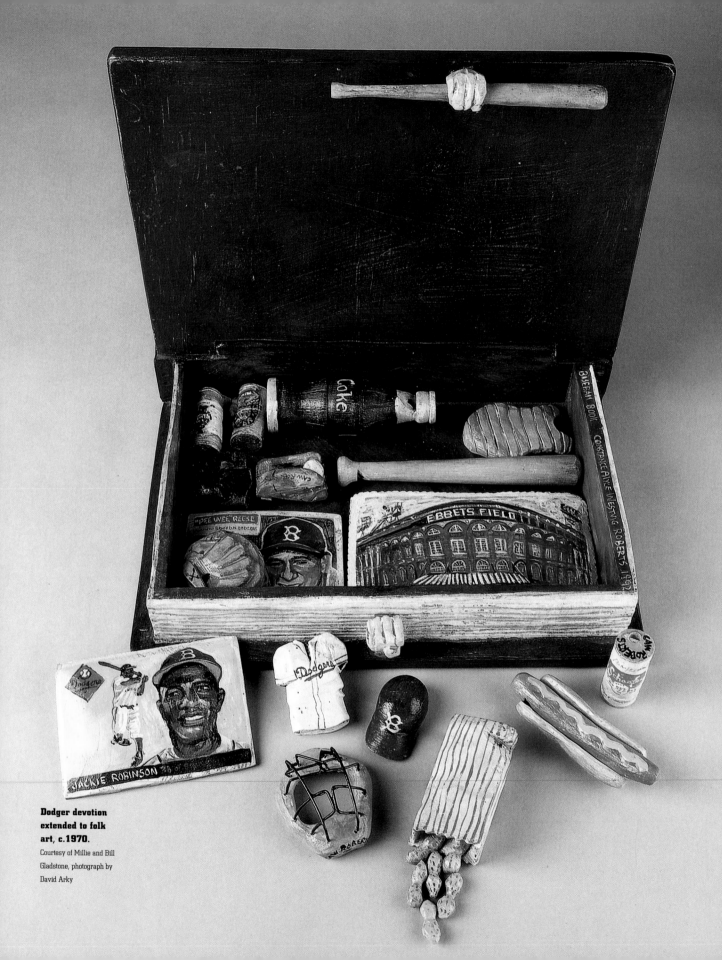

**Dodger devotion
extended to folk
art, c. 1970.**

Courtesy of Millie and Bill
Gladstone, photograph by
David Arky

The people in the streets and shops are often cruel. I can't remember a stranger ever congratulating me when the Giants won a game. But if we lose, a driver is sure to lean out the window of his car and yell across at us: "Wassa matter, you guys?"

— Giants manager
Leo Durocher

An intrepid photographer at Ebbets Field

Courtesy of the Barney Stein Photo Collection LLC, photograph by Barney Stein

Yankees and Dodgers warble on this 1951 record.

Courtesy of Bob and Adelyn Mayer, photograph by David Arky

Look! Listen! Learn! Baseball the Dodger way; book/record, 1956.

From the collection of Jerry Stern, photograph by David Arky

**Brooklyn Dodgers
Sym-phony Drum**
Courtesy of Gary Cypres,
photograph by Susan
Einstein, Los Angeles

> My rookie year signing autographs for Brooklyn kids made me feel like a bona fide major league player. I signed several, and then one boy came back a second time. In a few minutes, he was back for a third autograph. I asked him why he would want three of my autographs. "If I can get six of yours, I can trade them for one of Jackie Robinson's."
>
> CARL ERSKINE

When my children were young I used to read them a book called *Take Me Out to the Ball Game.* The words, of course, were the song's lyrics, spread over pages of drawings of Brooklyn in the time of the Dodgers. There were the requisite drawings of Ebbets Field and of the familiar faces. But the one that I found myself lingering over, too often delaying the turning of the page, was of a Brooklyn street scene—brownstones, stickball, and the Dodgers, presumably, on the radio. I can still summon in an instant that image of that place I never knew.

I missed talking about the Dodgers. I missed talking about a team that played in a tiny stadium that fostered the intimacy between the players and those who loved and (on bad days) hated them. I missed feeling a part of the conversation.

Brooklyn did lose something more than a baseball team when the Dodgers vanished. And because what was lost could not be quantified it was difficult to identify. As a result, the loss was described in ways that always felt too much, too painful, too traumatic. He tore out the heart…

But something vanished with the team and people knew it, and longed for it, even if they weren't exactly sure what it was.

We missed the talk. We missed each other.

> It never seemed that Giant fans were as involved emotionally or physically as some other fans. They never really affected a game at the Polo Grounds the way those fans at Ebbets Field could.
>
> RICHIE ASHBURN

INNING
5

The Giants-Dodgers Rivalry

Two Cheers for Horace Stoneham

Lee Lowenfish

The history books have not been very kind to Horace Charles Stoneham. At best, he has been credited for being one of the last owner–sportsmen in baseball, a man who at the age of 32 in 1936 inherited the New York Giants from his father Charles Abraham Stoneham and remained its primary owner for the next 40 years. It is true that the younger Stoneham has drawn some praise for his loyalty, keeping on the payroll longtime employees like Eddie Brannick, who joined the team in 1905 as a teenaged bat boy and served for decades as its road secretary; Hall of Fame slugger Mel Ott, who became his field manager; and Hall of Fame pitcher Carl Hubbell, who worked for many years as his farm director. However, Stoneham is remembered more for his legendary capacity for drink, a man whose companions sometimes had to climb out of windows to escape from long bibulous evenings. He has also drawn his share of calumny for his supporting role as Walter O'Malley's partner in the heisting of New York City's historic National League franchises to the more lucrative markets of California.

Yet there is another side to Horace Stoneham's baseball life that has been undeservedly neglected. Once Jackie Robinson's success in shattering the color line with the Dodgers was an unqualified success in 1947, Stoneham enthusiastically joined the cause of racially integrating the Giants. Not only did he sign many black players, including future Hall of Fame outfielders Monte Irvin and Willie Mays, but in an unprecedented

Facing page:
Joe Black, star relief pitcher of 1952
Private collection

> Once my father struck up a conversation with a priest we were sitting next to. He ended up buying beers for everyone in the whole area. There was that kind of feeling at Ebbets Field. Except when the Giants came. Then it was war.
>
> HERBY GREISSMAN,
> *It Happened in Brooklyn*, 1993

move, Stoneham also brought into his front-office team two noted personages from the Negro Leagues, Alejandro "Alex" Pompez and Frank Tidwillington Forbes. Their work in scouting and nurturing black talent played a significant behind-the-scenes role as the Giants, led on the field by manager Leo Durocher, won a pennant in 1951 and swept the World Series in 1954. The purpose of this essay is to give Horace Stoneham some long-overdue credit for his role in integrating not only the playing field but also the front office of the New York Giants franchise.

In 1948 Horace Stoneham became the first owner in baseball history to create a farm-club agreement with a Negro League team, Pompez's New York Cubans. In the colorful history of segregated black baseball, Pompez had been a major player. Born to a prosperous Havana cigar manufacturer in 1890, he was raised in Key West and Tampa, Florida, and moved to New York shortly before World War I. He made his first success with the New York Cuban Stars, a team that won the 1924 Eastern Colored League title and featured an emerging Martin Dihigo, a young Cuban who could play every position (including pitcher) and ultimately would be elected into baseball Halls of Fame in four countries—the United States, Cuba, Venezuela, and Puerto Rico.

The Eastern Colored League did not survive the 1920s, but Pompez kept the Cuban Stars alive as a barnstorming team that often played its home games in the Dyckman Oval, a ballpark located scarcely two miles north of the Stoneham family's

Giants program, 1951
Courtesy of Mike Santo

Giants program, 1955
Courtesy of Mike Santo

Dodgers program, 1956
Courtesy of Mike Santo

Ebbets Field "linen" postcard, c. 1950
Courtesy of Brian Strum

home park, the Polo Grounds. In 1930, five years before the Cincinnati Reds became the first major league team to introduce night baseball at Crosley Field, Pompez added lights to the Dyckman Oval. On big occasions, such as a 1935 exhibition in which the recently retired Babe Ruth played first base, the Oval drew overflow crowds approaching 10,000.

Unfortunately, Pompez's baseball business had been largely financed by his participation in the numbers racket, the illegal inner-city lottery that soared in popularity in the 1920s and '30s. Pompez's operation became so prosperous that it caught the attention of the notorious gangster Dutch Schultz. After Schultz's murder in 1935, crusading New York County district attorney Thomas Dewey (later the Governor of New York and a two-time U.S. presidential candidate) led a campaign to end corruption and illegal gambling. When Pompez learned that Dewey planned to indict him, he fled the country for almost two years, first to France and then to Mexico. In 1937, Pompez agreed to leave his haven south of the border and return to New York to testify for the state against the political accomplices of the Schultz operation. Friends feared for his safety, but he testified without incident in the summer of 1938 and soon resumed the operation of the New York Cubans.

With Dyckman Oval demolished, Pompez needed a home field for his team and Horace Stoneham gladly accepted him as a tenant at the Polo Grounds. Throughout

It was the rare kid in Brooklyn who wasn't a Dodger fan. They knew everything about them, felt so close to them. They called them by nicknames: Oisk for Erskine, Skoonj for Furillo, Ski for Hermanski, Cookie for Harry Lavagetto.

JOHN DOWNIE,

It Happened in Brooklyn, 1993

The Polo Grounds, stands filled on a sunny day; "linen" postcard c. 1950
From the collection of Bob Mayer

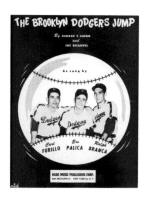

"The Brooklyn Dodgers Jump" also came out as a record in 1949. The Bruce Dorskind Collection, photograph by David Arky

NEW YORK'S FAMOUS BEER

WPIX·11

Best seats in the house, even if they are
483 feet away; center field, Polo Grounds

Courtesy of the National Baseball Hall of Fame Library,
Cooperstown, N.Y.

Our teachers had let us listen to the first two games on the radio. But I badly wanted to watch this culminating game. And I wanted to be in the sanctity of my home, sitting on the couch, my scorebook across my lap. Later, I discovered that more than half my classmates had failed to return to school that afternoon.

DORIS KEARNS GOODWIN

Brooklyn pennant
Courtesy of Hank Seiden,
photograph by David Arky

the 1940s the Cubans played their home games in the old ballpark on Coogan's Bluff when Stoneham's Giants were on the road. With the signing of Jackie Robinson in 1945 and his major league success in 1947, Pompez understood that survival would be difficult if not impossible for the segregated black leagues. According to historian Neil Lanctot, before the 1947 Negro League East–West All-Star game at the Polo Grounds, Pompez sent a letter to all the white major league owners inviting them to attend the game "to get a comprehensive line on the cream of Negro talent." Most of the owners declined Pompez's invitation, but Stoneham was so interested in Negro League talent that by 1948 he established his pioneer working agreement with the New York Cubans. The arrangement led to the Giants signing three of Pompez's veterans: Cuban-born catcher Ray Noble, third baseman Ray Dandridge, and pitcher Dave Barnhill. Noble made the Giants in 1951, but neither Dandridge nor Barnhill advanced beyond the Giants' top farm club in Minneapolis.

Carl Furillo, 1950 Bowman card
Courtesy of Kevin Bean

Stoneham grew to trust Pompez's evaluation of black and Hispanic talent. The Cuban scout approved of Stoneham's signing Monford Lee Irvin, who in January 1949 was purchased from the defunct Newark Eagles of the Negro National League. Born in Columbia, Alabama, and raised in nearby Orange, New Jersey, Irvin was a superior all-around athlete who in the late 1930s had set high-school records in baseball, football, and the javelin. Stoneham saw him play as a schoolboy and dreamed of signing him at the time. "I said it was too soon," the owner ruefully told Irvin after the hard-hitting outfielder had become a major league success. "I wish I had been braver."

Don Zimmer was one of many heirs apparent to Pee Wee Reese.
Courtesy of The "SPORT" Collection

Interestingly, Irvin almost became a Brooklyn Dodger on two separate occasions. Shortly after the war, Branch Rickey interviewed him as a possible candidate to break the color line, but the recently returned war veteran told him that he felt rusty. Unlike many established white major leaguers who had devoted their time in the war to

When Leo moved to the Polo Grounds, I am sure only a few of his Brooklyn admirers moved with him in spirit. Far worse was the fact that the Polo Grounds denizens refused to accept Leo. They had spent so many happy years booing him that it came as a shock to find that he was now on their side. Having considered the matter at some length, they decided to keep up the booing. Whenever Leo stepped out of the dugout, the air was filled with Bronx salutations. The team hit home runs, lost games, and struggled to keep in the first division. Leo was on the horns of a dilemma. The home-run hitters were great favorites in New York, but he felt they would never bring the Giants a pennant. He could keep them—and get booed; or he could trade them and possibly get murdered. LARAINE DAY

playing on military teams, Irvin had no such opportunity during his years as a soldier in Europe. He told Rickey that he needed time in Puerto Rican winter ball to get back into baseball shape. It did not take long for Irvin to regain his form, but for the next three seasons, he was limited to starring once again for the Newark Eagles and in the Cuban winter leagues.

When the Eagles folded after the 1948 season, the Dodgers contacted Irvin again and announced his signing early in January 1949. He was slated to report to their St. Paul farm team for spring training, but he told Rickey that he had signed a contract with Eagles owner Effa Manley for the upcoming season. Although the Eagles no longer in fact existed, Rickey told Irvin that he respected the reserve clause in his contract with Manley and released him from his commitment to Brooklyn. Stoneham quickly stepped in and signed Irvin along with two players from the Kansas City Monarchs—Hank Thompson, who had played briefly for the St. Louis Browns in 1947, and pitcher Ford Smith.

On July 8, 1949, Monte Irvin became the first African American to don the uniform of the New York Giants. He made his major league debut a few days before the All-Star Game in Brooklyn, which featured Dodger heroes Robinson, Roy Campanella, and Don Newcombe, as well as Cleveland's Larry Doby, the American League's first black player. A few days after the All-Star Game, Thompson made his National League debut. With the Polo Grounds located in the heart of west Harlem on 8th Avenue and 155th Street, Stoneham clearly had an economic incentive in bringing up black players for the local fans to cheer. He also had a fierce competitive motive, wanting to match his archrival Dodgers in the search for good black talent. Although Ford Smith never made the big leagues, the Giants owner was clearly committed to mining the newly opened market for black players. Dan Burley, a savvy black sports and entertainment writer, wrote approvingly that Stoneham may have been late to

Alvin Dark drew less fanfare than Reese or Rizzuto, perhaps unfairly. Courtesy of The "SPORT" Collection

Monte Irvin, 1951 Bowman card
Courtesy of Kevin Bean

Monte Irvin model glove, Trojan Pro Maker G71 Courtesy of Bob and Adelyn Mayer, photograph by David Arky

Monte Irvin, 1952 Bowman card
Courtesy of Kevin Bean

the integration cause but once he entered it, he jumped in with both feet. And his rival and partner, Branch Rickey, was happy to have the company and the competition.

The presence of Monte Irvin and Hank Thompson on the 1949 Giants did not pay immediate dividends. Thompson put up respectable numbers with a .280 batting average, .444 slugging average, and 9 home runs in 275 at-bats. Fighting injury, Irvin hit only .224 in 76 at-bats as the Giants finished a weak fifth, eight games under .500 and 24 games behind the pennant-winning Dodgers. But Durocher was beginning to take command of Stoneham's stumbling franchise that hadn't won a pennant since 1937. He had been unimpressed with previous power-laden Giants teams like the 1947 "Window Breakers" team that set a major league record with 221 home runs but still finished fourth because of a lack of speed and defense. Durocher convinced the paternal Stoneham to trade two key sluggers from that team, Sid Gordon and Willard Marshall, to the Boston Braves in exchange for Eddie Stanky and Alvin Dark, a brilliant double-play combination that could also win games with the bat.

In 1950 the Giants leaped to third place, 18 games over .500 and only five games behind the pennant-winning Philadelphia Phillies. Irvin started the season in Jersey City, the Giants' International League farm team, but after hitting over .500 with 10 home runs in 18 games, he returned to the Polo Grounds and established himself as a regular, playing first base and the outfield and hitting .299, with 15 home runs and 66 RBIs. Hank Thompson improved in every category: He hit .289 and slugged .463 with 20 home runs and 91 RBIs. But the year's most significant development for the future of the franchise happened far from the Polo Grounds.

In May 1950 the Giants farm system was in desperate need of a first baseman. Word came to Stoneham that Alonzo Powell of the Birmingham Black Barons might fit the bill. Alex Pompez's New York Cubans were playing the Black Barons in Alabama, and Stoneham asked his Latino associate to join some of his other scouts in appraising Powell's merits. As happens so often on these baseball missions, the eyes of the evaluators turned to someone else on the diamond. All agreed that the best prospect on the field was a 19-year-old center fielder who had been playing with the Barons since 1948. His name was Willie Howard Mays.

The Boston Braves were mildly interested in signing Mays, but they made an offer of $7,500 up front with another $7,500 if Mays delivered on the field. Stoneham, urged on by Pompez and his other scouts Ed Montague and Bill Harris, offered $10,000 outright for Mays' contract, and the deal with the Black Barons was struck. The young Mays had to miss his high-school prom because his orders were to report immediately to Class B Trenton of the Interstate League. At first, Mays struggled in his new surroundings, going 0-for-22. However, his defense was immediately out-

Left to Right:
Monte Irvin, 1953 Bowman card
Courtesy of Kevin Bean

Monte Irvin, 1954 Topps card
Courtesy of Kevin Bean

Monte Irvin, 1955 Topps card
Courtesy of Kevin Bean

standing as he displayed his enviable range and powerful arm. Soon his offense came around, and he was on his way upward in professional baseball.

During Mays' first road game with Trenton in Hagerstown, Maryland, the center fielder was thrust into the role of pioneer when he became the first African American athlete to play on the hitherto segregated diamonds of the small western-Maryland city. Mays endured a barrage of racist epithets from the crowd, but it didn't hinder his play. Before the last game of the series, a chastened local paper headlined, "Do Not Disturb Mays." In an interview Mays gave to the Baseball Hall of Fame over fifty years later, he remembered warmly the gesture of three of his teammates, Bob Easterwood, Herb Perelto, and Hank Rowland, who came to spend the night with him in his hotel in the segregated part of town, volunteering to protect him.

In 1951 Mays rose to the Giants' top farm team, the Minneapolis Millers of the American Association. He was hitting a robust .477 when he got the call in late May to report to the struggling parent club in Philadelphia. Losers of 11 in a row early in the season, the Giants were under .500 and management was fearful of falling irreversibly behind the Dodgers. Yet in a gesture of benevolent understanding, Horace Stoneham took out an advertisement in a Minneapolis paper expressing his regret that he was taking away such an exciting player. "We appreciate his worth to the Millers, [but Mays'] merit must be rewarded," Stoneham wrote.

Mays' career in the big leagues started slowly as he made the adjustment to top-flight pitching. Inserted immediately by Durocher into the third slot in the lineup,

About baseball loyalties, the Giants were playing the Dodgers, and we were all surprised at an old colored man who was riding Jackie Robinson unmercifully. "That's a man of your race, why are you so hard on Jackie?" protested a neighbor. "I wouldn't care if he was Booker T. Washington. I want the Giants to win."
LARAINE DAY

Hank Thompson, slugging third baseman, in the 1954 World Series Courtesy of The "SPORT" Collection

Mays went 0-for-12 in his first appearances. After he got his first major league hit, a long home run off Warren Spahn at the Polo Grounds, another drought of 0-for-13 followed. The disconsolate rookie began to wonder if he belonged in the big leagues, but Leo Durocher, his protector and biggest fan, kept him in the lineup.

In another gesture of paternal benevolence, Stoneham assigned his scout Frank Forbes to be Mays' off-field guardian. One of Forbes' first acts was to find housing for Mays in the rooming house of Mrs. Anne Goosby, an Alabama native who provided the kind of home cooking young Willie had thrived on growing up near Birmingham. She saw that Mays got plenty of sleep after his frequent games of stickball with the neighborhood kids. She also tried to control his addiction to soda pop, but admitted, "The only thing I can't stop him from doing is those comic books. He sure has a lot of them."

Forbes took it upon himself to keep as many doting females away from the irrepressible Mays as possible. Mays' roommate on the road was family man Monte Irvin, who found rooming with Mays like having a kid brother who always loved to wrestle with him. But the older veteran was impressed by Willie's taste for fine clothes that he never allowed to be wrinkled.

The numbers from Mays' first big-league season in 1951 were not overwhelming. But his ebullient presence on the field and in the clubhouse lifted the Giants into a dominant force that roared from 13-and-a-half games behind in mid-August to win the 1951 pennant on Bobby Thomson's dramatic home run in the final inning of a three-game playoff against the Dodgers. "Mays can help a team just by riding the bus with them," rival National League manager Charlie Grimm marveled. Branch Rickey, now running the Pittsburgh Pirates, said, "The secret to Willie Mays is the frivolity in his bloodstream."

The Giants lost the World Series in six games to the Yankees in 1951, but not before they provided several thrills for their fans and threw a scare into their opponents. Irvin in particular had a great series, going 11-for-24 and stealing home in the Game 1 victory. Mays was held in check, going 4-for-22, and Thompson was only 2-for-14; but clearly the black players on the Giants had shown they were outstanding major league contributors.

In his unique way, Durocher made his own statement on behalf of integration. Because of an injury to Don Mueller in the final playoff game, Durocher started Thompson in right field for Game 1. With Irvin in left and Mays in center, the Giants sent out to the field a baseball first—an all-black outfield. "Looks kinda dark out there, doesn't it?" the manager quipped to a reporter. Earlier in the season, Durocher inserted black shortstop Artie Wilson as a late-inning replacement for Alvin Dark in a

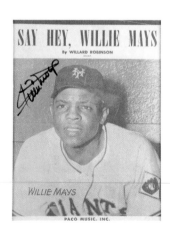

Willie Mays autographed sheet music, 1954

The Bruce Dorskind Collection, photograph by David Arky

**Leo Durocher and Willie Mays,
spring training 1955**

Museum of the City of New York, LOOK Collection,
photograph by Earl Theisen

**Pee Wee Reese model glove,
Olympic #334** Courtesy of Bob and
Adelyn Mayer, photograph by David Arky

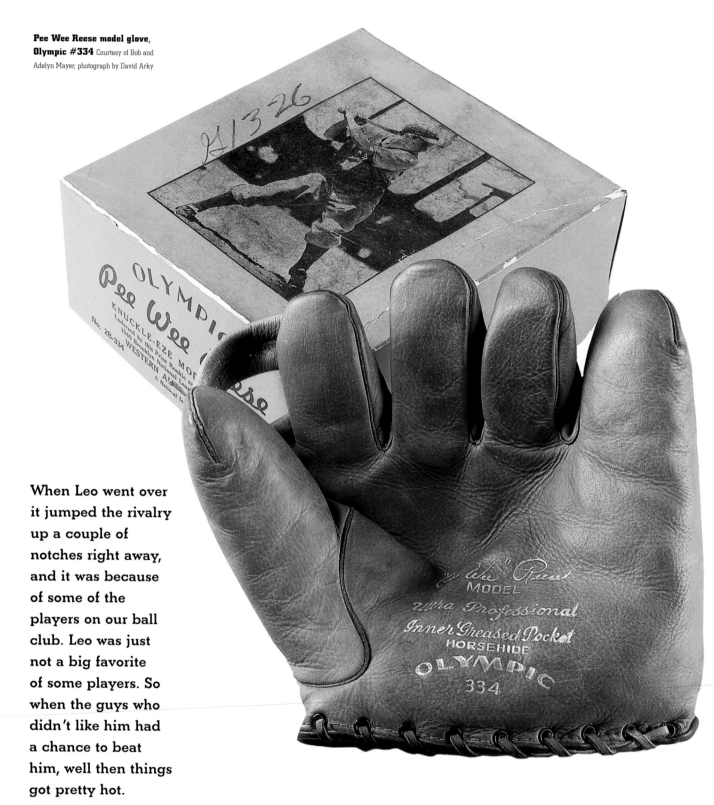

When Leo went over
it jumped the rivalry
up a couple of
notches right away,
and it was because
of some of the
players on our ball
club. Leo was just
not a big favorite
of some players. So
when the guys who
didn't like him had
a chance to beat
him, well then things
got pretty hot.
PEE WEE REESE

rout over the St. Louis Cardinals. With Ray Noble subbing for Wes Westrum behind the plate, Monte Irvin at first base and Hank Thompson at third base, the Giants had four black players in the field, the first time any major league team had played so many non-white athletes at the same time. In the early years of baseball integration, there was already an unspoken rule about not playing more than three players of color at the same time; but Durocher's gesture was his way of saying that he didn't care about quotas, but only winning ballgames and giving all players a chance. In a decision likely taken above the manager's head, Artie Wilson was farmed out when Mays came up. The Giants never gave the future Hall of Famer Ray Dandridge even a cup of coffee in the big leagues, citing his age and their preference for the far younger Hank Thompson. Nonetheless, it seemed that Durocher had Stoneham's team headed in a positive and truly interracial direction.

However, before the Giants even had a chance to start their defense of the pennant, disaster struck in an April 1952 exhibition game against the Cleveland Indians in Denver, Colorado. Running from first base on a single to right field by Willie Mays, Monte Irvin broke his ankle sliding into third base. It was an unnecessary slide because the throw from the outfield had been cut off. Mays wept inconsolably, blaming himself for getting the hit that led to Irvin's injury. Not only was the valuable Irvin lost for most of the season, but Mays was called into the military in late May, not to return to the team until the 1954 season.

Without the injured Irvin and the departed Mays, Durocher still would not let the team quit. The Giants finished second in 1952, a respectable four-and-a-half games behind the pennant-winning Dodgers. But in 1953, Brooklyn came out of the gates sizzling, and the Giants fell to fifth, 14 games under .500 and 35 games out of first. Polo Grounds attendance, which in 1951 had soared over a million for the first time since the record-setting season of 1947, fell to 811,000. In two seasons the Giants had lost more than a quarter million paying customers.

Prospects brightened when Mays was discharged from the Army at the beginning of the 1954 exhibition season. When he arrived in Phoenix, Leo Durocher immediately inserted him into the lineup. All Mays did was make a great catch on his first chance in the field and hit a home run in his first at-bat. It was a happy omen for the coming season, in which Mays would hit .345, win the Most Valuable Player Award, and lead the Giants to a pennant and a four-game sweep of the Cleveland Indians, who had won 111 regular-season games. Mays' game-saving catch in the eighth inning of the first game set the tone for the entire World Series even though he went only 4-for-14 at the plate. With obscure utility outfielder Jim "Dusty" Rhodes providing game-winning home runs in the first two games, Mays' bat was not needed.

As far as my father was concerned, the greatest betrayal since Judas's kiss took place in midseason, 1948. The Giants fired the idol of all Giant fans, Mel Ott, and replaced him with the most hated Dodger of all time, Leo "The Lip" Durocher.

JACK McCORMACK

Verbal razzing wasn't the only way to get on a rookie. We went into Ebbets Field for a series early in the season when I was still playing second. In those days, we used to throw our gloves down at the end of the inning, leave them right out on the field. Whenever I came back onto the field that day I couldn't find my glove. It was never where I left it and I'd always spot it way out in right field. This went on for a couple of innings and I began to wonder what was going on. The next time we got them out I ran like hell to the dugout and then turned around real fast. There was Eddie Stanky, the Dodgers' second baseman, kicking my glove all the way to the right field bullpen. It was a typical Stanky ploy, showing his contempt for a rookie. It was also my introduction to the Brat, a guy who would be an important teammate of mine a few years later. BOBBY THOMSON

But 1954 would be the last hurrah for the New York Giants. Although they drew over 1,115,000 fans, that number was almost a half-million shy of their record-setting season of 1947. The Dodgers came out flying in 1955 and would romp to the pennant by 13-and-a-half games over the second-place Milwaukee Braves. The Giants were 18-and-a-half games back in third, only six games over .500. Before the midpoint of the 1955 season, the 36-year-old Irvin was released, and during the last week of the season Durocher resigned as manager. He evidently saw the looming disintegration of the franchise, its lack of new talent, white or black, and a sadly crumbling ballpark. Attendance fell nearly 300,000, back to 1953 levels, with 30–40 percent of the total coming from the 11 annual visits of the hated Dodgers.

Even more alarming to the future of the denizens of the Polo Grounds, Stoneham paid a visit to Minneapolis during the 1955 season and openly talked about relocating the Giants once his lease ran its course in 1962. By 1957 Walter O'Malley would convince Stoneham to speed up his timetable and change his destination.

Alex Pompez stayed in Stoneham's employ as they prepared to move west. During the Giants' last seasons in New York, Pompez was directly responsible for the signing of future Hall of Famers pitcher Juan Marichal and first basemen Orlando Cepeda and Willie McCovey. With his Cuban ancestry and knowledge of Latin America, Pompez watched over the Latino players with the solicitude that Frank Forbes had shown Willie Mays. It is a fitting conclusion to remember that both Pompez and Forbes had been hired by the same man — Horace Stoneham — who understood from a lifetime in baseball the need for sympathetic understanding and care in the most demanding and humbling of sports.

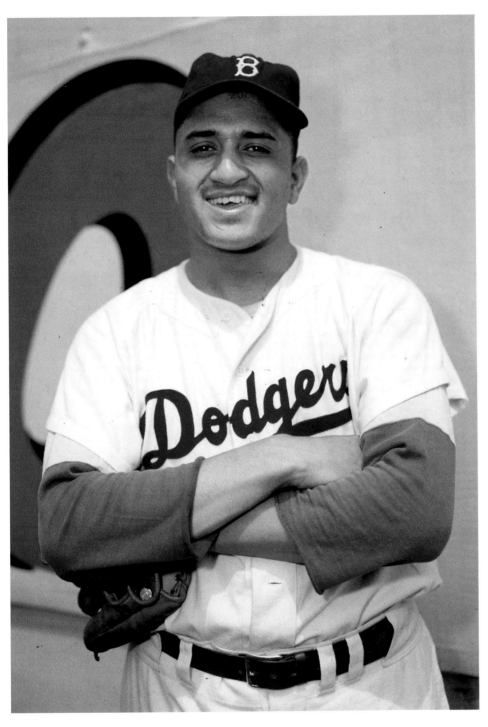

Don Newcombe
Courtesy of The "SPORT" Collection

Dramatic and fateful as was the Sisler tenth-inning home run to close out the Dodgers in '50, baseball offers no more dramatic and fateful a crusher than the Bobby Thomson ninth-inning homer at the Polo Grounds that closed out the Dodgers in '51. The Giants overcame a big Brooklyn lead in the fall of '51 and on the last day of the race won quickly at Boston. The Dodgers were behind in their game at Philadelphia when the scoreboard showed the Giants' success. Brooklyn had to beat the Phillies to tie New York, and the Dodgers did in one of the game's highly memorable affairs that went into the darkness. Robinson saved it once with a great diving catch, and then won it in the fourteenth inning with a home run.
RED BARBER

The Media
My America

George Vecsey

This is my earliest childhood memory of baseball in New York.

My father had worked at the *Daily News* during the war but was displaced by the returning servicemen. He was temporarily working as a special-delivery mailman, driving around Queens, circumventing abandoned rail lines and remaining farmland, with baskets of mail stacked on the seats.

As often as I could get away with it on schooldays, I came up with strange medical symptoms until my father would stick me with the excess packages as he made his rounds. With three baseball teams in New York, there was often a game on the radio.

If the crisp southern voice of Red Barber was not available on the Dodgers' station, we would go slumming and listen to our blood enemies, the Giants, or else the dreaded Yankees, with Mel Allen's booming Alabama drawl fretting over DiMaggio's sore heel or some other calamity. I spent my formative years shouting, "Shut up, Mel," at the radio, learning many years later that he was one of the more gentle souls in the business.

We were a newspaper family. My father, who was working part-time at the *Daily News* at night, used to tell me about the brash reporter named Dick Young who was doing a great job covering the Dodgers.

The postwar period was a golden age on the field in New York, and also a time of giants in the media. In many towns, the local writers and broadcasters were expected to "root, root, root for the home team," but in New York they were expected to sound more neutral. Dick Young was a reporter, but he was also a harsh critic.

Facing page:
Graham MacNamee, pioneer baseball announcer
Private collection

1950s radio: Can't you hear Red Barber now? From the collection of Angela and Thomas Sarro, photograph by David Arky

Dodgers press pin, 1947 World Series Originally owned by Mr. Christie Bohnsack, Museum of the City of New York, gift of Olga Lewando, photograph by David Arky

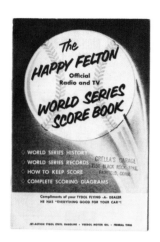

Happy Felton giveaway from Tydol Flying A gasoline

From the collection of Jerry Stern

The sportswriters, more than any other group or individual, are responsible for the entry of Negro players into organized baseball. For years and years they have fought for the abolishment of the color line. Never have they let baseball's officialdom forget that as long as they barred any race, creed, or color from the diamond, baseball could not be called the American sport.

JACKIE ROBINSON

In 1948, while the Dodgers were falling apart in the pennant race, Young referred to the popular book and movie, *A Tree Grows in Brooklyn.* His lead sentence one day was: "The tree that grew in Brooklyn was an apple tree," a reference to the Dodgers' inability to swallow—"choking up," as the ballplayers called it.

Through Dick Young, we learned about the strategies on the field, the patois of the clubhouse. He was the first modern baseball writer, dragging reporters and broadcasters, fans and players, along with him.

New York was divided into three bristling camps in those wonderful days, with Giants fans still carrying the hauteur of the first quarter of the century, when the Giants appealed to the carriage trade. The Yankees, immigrants from Baltimore at the turn of the century, now swaggered after their first hundred pennants. The Dodgers, long a collection of bumblers, had been rebuilt by Branch Rickey in the early 1940s, and were about to embark on an epic decade. With 22 games between the teams, Giants fans and Dodgers fans bickered all season long.

"You'd come out of Ebbets Field after a game and fans would be standing around arguing," recalled Jack Lang, who began covering the Dodgers for the *Long Island Press* in 1946.

"They wouldn't fight," Lang added in 2006. "But they would definitely argue." Half a century later, he recalled leaving the Polo Grounds after a Dodgers–Giants game, along with Barney Kremenko, who covered the Giants for the *Journal–American*, and Kremenko's lovely wife, Gerry.

A fan trailed Kremenko, repeatedly asking him who was the better defensive catcher, the Dodgers' Roy Campanella or the Giants' Wes Westrum. Kremenko was ignoring the fan, until his wife prodded him, "Barney, answer the man." Kremenko shrugged expressively, as only he could, and said, "Westrum," to which the fan responded, "What the heck do you know?" How New York is that?

In that ancient world of day games and rudimentary television, a large percentage of New Yorkers still read morning papers at home or on their way to work, and, when they headed home, a whole new assortment of PM papers was being hawked on street corners or home-delivered by urchins on bicycles.

When Lang started traveling with the Dodgers in 1946, ten or more newspapers sent reporters on the road (subsidized by the clubs, a practice no longer permitted). There were the four morning papers: the *Daily Mirror,* the *Daily News,* the *Herald Tribune,* and the *Times;* and three afternoon papers: the *World–Telegram and Sun,* the *Journal–American,* and the *Post* (long before it became an Australian-language paper under Rupert Murdoch). In addition, there was the venerable *Long Island Press* and soon the growing giant from Long Island, *Newsday.* The *Brooklyn Eagle*—Walt Whit-

**Casey Stengel
charms the
reporters, 1956.**
Museum of the City of New
York, LOOK Collection,
photograph by Arnold
Newman

OTANY

BurmaShave

LIFEBUOY

PHILIP
MORRIS

GEM

457 FT.

Dumont TV
cameramen shoot
World Series
action at Yankee
Stadium.
Private Collection

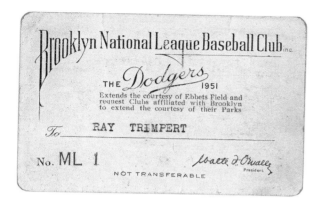

Brooklyn National League Baseball Club, Inc.

THE *Dodgers* 1951

Extends the courtesy of Ebbets Field and
request Clubs affiliated with Brooklyn
to extend the courtesy of their Parks

To RAY TRIMPERT

No. ML 1

Walter F. O'Malley
President

NOT TRANSFERABLE

N. Y. YANKEES
STADIUM CLUB

is pleased to extend guest privileges to

Mr. Mel Allen

1952

John J. Bergen
Chairman

Francis T. Hunter
PRESIDENT

Brooklyn National League Baseball Club, Inc.

THE *Dodgers* 1948

EXTEND THE COURTESY OF
EBBETS FIELD

To Sid Lohenfeld

WORKING PRESS

No. 281

Branch Rickey
& Pres.

NOT TRANSFERABLE

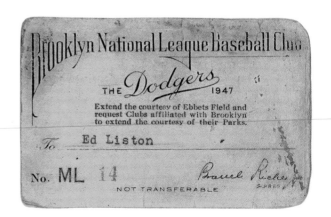

The American League Baseball Club of N. Y., Inc.

Season Pass - 1947

Yankees

Mr.

No.

PRESIDENT

This pass is issued subject to the terms and conditions printed on reverse side hereof.

NEW YORK GIANTS
POLO GROUNDS PRESS CLUB
1957

Jim Taylor

MEMBER

Dayton Journal-Herald

AFFILIATION

Garry Schumacher

COUNTERSIGNED

Brooklyn National League Baseball Club

THE *Dodgers* 1947

Extend the courtesy of Ebbets Field and
request Clubs affiliated with Brooklyn
to extend the courtesy of their Parks.

To Ed Liston

No. ML 14

Branch Rickey
& Pres.

NOT TRANSFERABLE

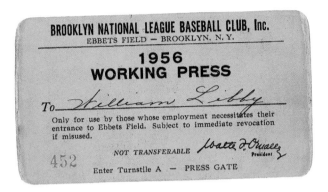

BROOKLYN NATIONAL LEAGUE BASEBALL CLUB, Inc.
EBBETS FIELD — BROOKLYN, N. Y.

1956
WORKING PRESS

To *William Libby*

Only for use by those whose employment necessitates their
entrance to Ebbets Field. Subject to immediate revocation
if misused.

452   NOT TRANSFERABLE   *Walter F. O'Malley*
President

Enter Turnstile A — PRESS GATE

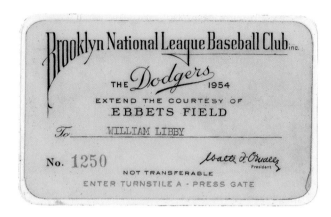

Brooklyn National League Baseball Club, inc.

THE *Dodgers* 1954

EXTEND THE COURTESY OF
EBBETS FIELD

To   WILLIAM LIBBY

No. 1250   NOT TRANSFERABLE   *Walter F. O'Malley*
President

ENTER TURNSTILE A - PRESS GATE

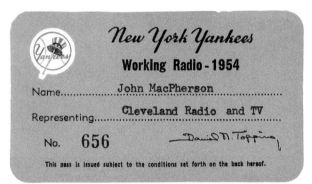

New York Yankees

Working Radio - 1954

Name.................... John MacPherson

Representing............ Cleveland Radio and TV

No.   656   *Daniel R. Topping*

This pass is issued subject to the conditions set forth on the back hereof.

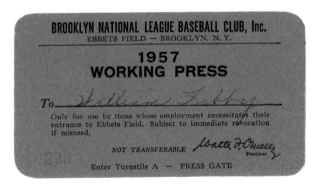

BROOKLYN NATIONAL LEAGUE BASEBALL CLUB, Inc.
EBBETS FIELD — BROOKLYN, N. Y.

1957
WORKING PRESS

To *William Libby*

Only for use by those whose employment necessitates their
entrance to Ebbets Field. Subject to immediate revocation
if misused.

NOT TRANSFERABLE   *Walter F. O'Malley*
President

Enter Turnstile A — PRESS GATE

1947
WORLD SERIES
Yankee Stadium — New York City

MESSENGER
MUTUAL TELEVISION

Holder of Ticket Entitled Also to
Field Privileges at
YANKEE STADIUM
This Badge Must Be Worn Where It
Can Be Seen At All Times

Game   2   X

(Enter at Press Gate)

1953
WORLD SERIES
Yankee Stadium — New York City

REPORTER
North Adams
Transcript

Is Granted Field and Stand Priv-
ileges Subject to Rules of the
OFFICE OF THE
BASEBALL COMMISSIONER
This Badge Must Be Worn Where It
Can Be Seen At All Times

Games   267XX

NOT GOOD IN PRESS BOX
(Enter at Press Gate)

**Various passes for working
press of all three teams,
including Mel Allen's for 1952**
Courtesy of Mike Santo

**Working press passes for
Yankee Stadium, 1947 and
1953 World Series**
From the collection of Jerry Stern

Dodgers World Series press pin, 1949 Originally owned by Mr. Christie Bohnsack, Museum of the City of New York, gift of Olga Lewando, photograph by David Arky

The beer and the ball team, both vanished from New York.
Private collection

> In my house, no one read any paper from the front to the back. The sports news began on the back page, and the Jewish papers were read from back to front: the *Tag*, the *Forward*, the *Morning Journal*. The candy store on McDonald Avenue also sold the *Freiheit*, the Jewish communist newspaper, under the counter.
>
> MIRIAM KITTRELL,
> *It Happened in Brooklyn*, 1993

man's paper—also sent a reporter on the road until its demise in March 1955, with impeccable timing, missing the Dodgers' grand single championship. Occasionally the two Newark papers, the *News* and the *Star–Ledger*, traveled too. The size of the traveling cadre was about the same for the Giants and Yankees.

The baseball reporters, all male back then, came in many ages and sizes and levels of intelligence, but one writer stood out among them. Dick Young had grown up in the Washington Heights section of Manhattan, had been a Giants fan, and had covered the Giants for a while during the war, when he was exempt from service because of his growing family. In 1946, he switched to the Dodgers.

Young carried the banner for the *Daily News*, which had the largest daily circulation in American history—over 2.4 million on weekdays and a peak Sunday circulation of 4.7 million in 1947. Its slogan was "New York's Picture Newspaper," but it also carried snappy headlines, pungent writing, and frequent moralizing, along with juicy chunks of scandal.

"Our paper has four times as many readers; not brokers and bank presidents, but you know what Lincoln said, 'He made so many of them,'" Young said in 1952, in a savage indoctrination speech to Roger Kahn, a young reporter with the *Trib*. Young

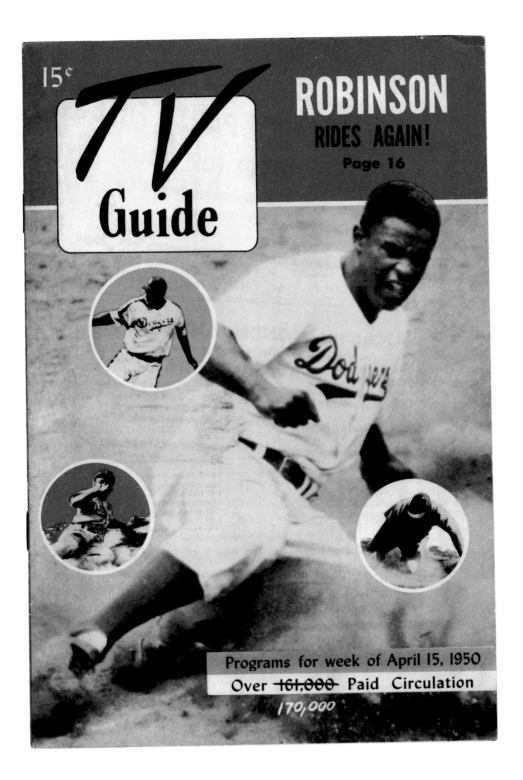

Yogi and Yoo-Hoo, a memorable pairing

Private collection

"TV Guide,"
April 15, 1950

From the collection of
Jerry Stern

Mickey Mantle
and portraitist
Bob Sandberg
Museum of the City of
New York, LOOK Collection,
photograph by Edie

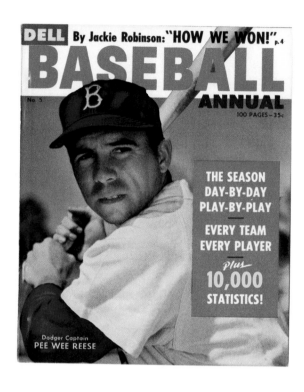

Those newspapers gave a real portrayal of what was going on. If a player didn't perform well, the writers traveling with the team did not try to smooth it over. They would write, "He's a bum; he's got to go today." They'd try to stir something up. It helped to build up the rivalry between the teams. The players all read the papers.

MONTE IRVIN

Clockwise from Left:
"Pocket Television Theatre," a Jackie Robinson flip book
Courtesy of Brain Strum, photograph by David Arky

"Baseball Annual" with Pee Wee Reese
From the collection of Jerry Stern

Street and Smith's 1947 "Baseball Yearbook"
From the collection of Jerry Stern

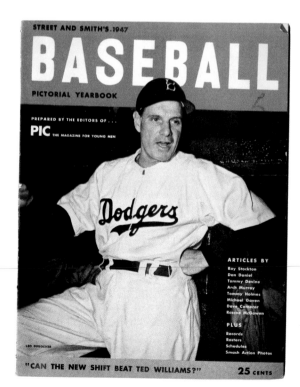

would later become one of the most compelling figures in Kahn's classic book about the Dodgers, *The Boys of Summer*.

"I'll kill you, kid," Young warned Kahn, presumably meaning he would outwork him. Then Young gave him a quick lesson: "…Now you're gonna write the games most of the time. Nothing you can do about that and it ain't bad. But anytime, you hear me, anytime you can get your story off the game you got to do it. Because that's unusual and people read unusual things. Fights. Bean balls. Whatever. Write them, not the game."

Up to then, there had been two schools of sports writing. One was Fustian and Whim Wham, as H.L. Mencken called flowery phrases and grand allegories, perhaps from the southern influence of Grantland Rice and other transplants who adapted the once-a-week hyperbole of college football to the gritty daily soap opera of baseball. The other style was from the Von Clausewitz School, which turned each game into the Battle of Waterloo, with a runner trying to steal second base becoming as weighty as a flanking maneuver by Prussian cavalry.

Young demystified this murky stuff. In his world, ballplayers spat tobacco juice and cursed and second-guessed the manager. He backed it up with quotes. Up to then, sportswriters had generally acted as imperious historians, writing from on high, but Young bustled down from the press box, entered the clubhouse, and chatted up the ballplayers. Carl Furillo, not the swiftest of runners, became known as "Skoonj" as in scungilli—Italian for snail. Young employed dugout phrases like "ribbie," a term for RBI or run batted in. After Young had scooped indolent reporters once too often, their bosses delivered an ultimatum, which could be boiled down to, "Don't let that SOB out of your sight."

It wasn't hard to notice Young. He wore sport coats, with either a flashy tie or the top couple of buttons open on his shirt, to reveal a deep tan, his wavy hair artfully combed, a cigar in his mouth, which did not hinder his grating voice. In their annual winter dinner, the baseball writers would perform skits, and Young would drape his sport jacket over his shoulder, and perform a Sinatra parody. Perfect. Now that they are both gone, Sinatra and Young merge in my mind.

And he was loud. Lord, was he loud. He could chuckle and praise and use clubhouse nicknames—Pee Wee Reese, the Dodgers' leader from Kentucky, was "Captain." He was also fearless. Duke Snider, the gifted, tempestuous center fielder, once threatened to beat up a sportswriter who had criticized him. Up close, Young advised Snider to concentrate on hitting baseballs rather than old men.

Young was viciously competitive—but he was also generous. In 1956, Don Larsen, the Yankees' carouser and underachiever, pitched the only perfect game in the history

**"Who's Who in the Big Leagues,"
1956, with Campy on cover**
From the collection of Jerry Stern

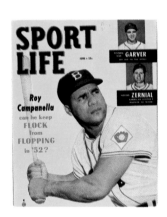

"Sport Life" with Campy on cover
From the collection of Jerry Stern

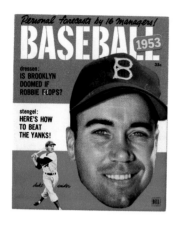

"Baseball 1953" with Duke Snider

From the collection of Jerry Stern

One of the men who fought doggedly for the entry of Negroes into the ranks of organized baseball was the late and beloved Damon Runyon. Probably the most gifted sportswriter of our time, Runyon abhorred the ban against Negro players. For instance, in May of 1945, before I was signed by Montreal, he wrote: "I read a statement in a newspaper the other day that baseball belongs to all the people. This may be true of baseball as a vacant-lot pastime, but it is definitely not true of organized or professional baseball, and it is sheer hypocrisy to say that it does. If baseball belonged to all the people and the people had a vote in its conduct, Negroes would be permitted to play in organized baseball if they could make good by the same standards set for the whites." JACKIE ROBINSON

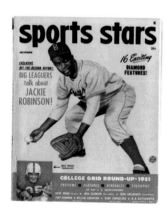

"Sports Stars" with Jackie on cover

From the collection of Jerry Stern

Jackie Robinson Wheaties Ad

From the collection of Jerry Stern

1956 Baseball Schedule
From the collection of Jerry Stern

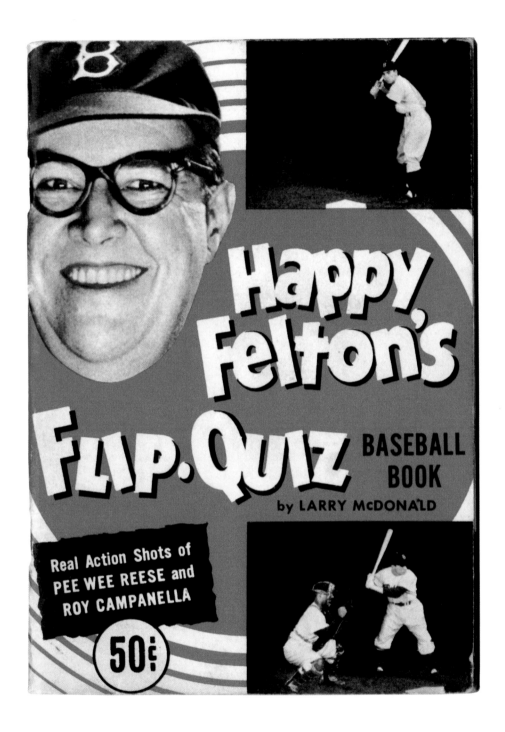

**Happy Felton's flip
quiz book**
Courtesy of Brian Strum

In order to be sure he gave the score often enough to keep the fans updated about the game, Red used a regular kitchen egg timer in the booth. It took three minutes for the sand to run through the glass tube, so Red would give the score and then turn the timer over to run through again.

CARL ERSKINE

of current affairs and features. In 1948, the morning papers were the *Times, Herald Tribune, Daily News,* and *Mirror*. The *Times* and *Trib* were a nickel, the *News* and *Mirror,* two cents. The afternoon papers were the *Sun, Journal American, World Telegram* and *Post*. There were others: the *Compass, PM;* the Yiddish papers were also very strong. Most people read at least two papers a day.

LEONARD KOPPETT,
It Happened in Manhattan, 2001

In His Big League Debut
JACKIE SCORES WINNING RUN

Here are some of the fans who crowded Ebbets Field in Brooklyn to see Jackie Robinson as he made his debut with the Dodgers.

Jackie Robinson looks to the future.

Robbie's Bunt Turns Tide

By WENDELL SMITH, Courier Sports Editor

PRESS BOX, Ebbets Field, Brooklyn, N. Y.—Playing his first big league game of the 1947 National League season, Jackie Robinson came romping home from second base here Tuesday afternoon with what proved to be the Brooklyn Dodgers, winning run while 26,623 fans roared hilariously ...nd the Boston Braves went down to defeat, 5 to 3.

Police Halt Flareup at Chapel Hill

By LEN GRAVES Jr.
(Pittsburgh Courier Press Service)

CHAPEL HILL, N. C.—Last This sleepy little Piedmont Village, regarded far and wide as the "citadel of democracy in the South," and seat of the University of North Carolina, became a scene of sudden mob violence here late Sunday afternoon as taxicab drivers and young hoodlums assaulted an interracial group of young lecturers at the Chapel Hill Bus Station and then threatened to burn down the home of a liberal white Presbyterian minister in which the interracial group took refuge.

WASHINGTON
pittsburgh Courier
EDITION of

VOL. XXXVIII—No. 16   PITTSBURGH, PA., SATURDAY, APRIL 19, 1947   PRICE TWELVE CENTS

Packs 'Em In
Jackie Now 'Darling of The Brooks'

By WENDELL SMITH
(Courier Sports Editor)

Big Day for Dodgers

Wears Big '42'
Robinson Mobbed by Cameramen and Fans At Historic Opener

By WENDELL SMITH, Courier Sports Editor

BROOKLYN—History was made here Tuesday afternoon in Brooklyn's flag-bedecked, sun-kissed Ebbets Field when smiling JACKIE ROBINSON trotted out on the greenswept diamond with the rest of his Dodger teammates and played first base in the opening game of the 1947 National League season against Boston's battling Braves.

Robinson's Game Record

By WENDELL SMITH

Conductor Exonerated
Slain Man's Family May Sue Railroad

By A. M. RIVERA Jr.
(Staff Correspondent)

SMITHFIELD, N. C.—The U. S. Supreme Court's ignominiously repudiated here last week when a coroner's jury exonerated Atlantic Coast Line conductor C. A. James for killing Fletcher But Melvin, a 21-year-old Negro passenger traveling to interstate. Melvin refused to comply with State Jim-crow regulations.

Wesley Won't Be Forced Out

AKA's Pledge White Student

Dining Car Suit Dismissed

Jackie Romps Home From Second Base As 26,000 Cheer

By WENDELL SMITH, Courier Sports Editor

EBBETS FIELD, Brooklyn, N. Y.—Here is the play by play account of the Brooklyn-Boston big league opener as played here Tuesday afternoon before a crowd of 26,623.

Nashville Lawyer Seeks City Post

Primaries Open to Negroes in Macon, Ga.

How The Courier Covered The Jackie Robinson Story

Your Public Conduct
If you have a gripe, leave it at home

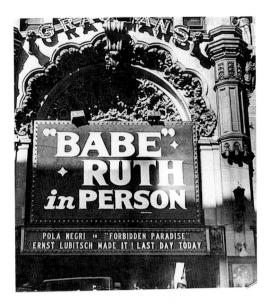

of the World Series: 27 Dodgers up, 27 Dodgers down. Young noticed his *Daily News* colleague, Joe Trimble, facing a blank page in his portable typewriter. This was worrisome, since Trimble was expected to turn in the lead article very soon. Young handed Trimble a sheet containing seven words: "The imperfect man pitched a perfect game." Trimble took it from there. Young never mentioned his kind deed until Trimble told the story decades later during a tribute to Young.

In his early days, Young was a liberal, a champion of union activity, a supporter of racial equality. Once Jackie Robinson began to show his fiery side, he and Young butted heads, inevitably.

Young was hardly the only star in the sports pages of that time. Some of the others were Jimmy Cannon, Milton Gross, Joe Williams, Dan Parker, Dan Daniel, Harold Rosenthal, Red Smith, Arthur Daley, Frank Graham, Tom Meany, and Dave Anderson, plus Stan Isaacs and Jack Mann of *Newsday*.

It was a time of transition, with newspaper circulation about to falter. The three New York teams had resisted radio coverage until late in the 1930s because management thought free broadcasts would cut into ticket sales. Now radio had a hold on the fans, who argued the relative merits of Mel Allen and Red Barber the same way they argued over the Yankees shortstop, Phil Rizzuto, or his Dodgers counterpart, Pee Wee Reese.

Jackie Robinson debut, reported in "Pittsburgh Courier," Washington edition, Saturday, April 19, 1947 Library of Congress

Allen, from the University of Alabama, had a way of glorifying the Yankee players, calling Joe DiMaggio "The Yankee Clipper," Tommy Henrich "Old Reliable," and the diminutive Phil Rizzuto

> **On afternoons when both the Dodgers and the Yankees were playing an afternoon game, we set our dueling radios on opposite sides of the blanket, the warm voice of Red Barber issuing from one end of the blanket, the harsh, tinny voice of Mel Allen from the other.**
> DORIS KEARNS GOODWIN

Three Yankees press pins from championship seasons

Originally owned by Mr. Christie Bohnsack, Museum of the City of New York, gift of Olga Lewando, photograph by David Arky

In 1947, an innovation changed the character of the neighborhood somewhat. Stores selling television sets opened on Franklin Avenue. Most families found the cost of these small black and white sets prohibitive. Soon, it was not unusual to see people carrying beach chairs strolling down the avenue on an evening, setting them up in front of the store window.

MEYER L. BLOCK

"Scooter." Allen's signature phrases were "Going, going, gone" for a home-run call and "How about that?" in response to a great play or a strange play, and he could go on in great detail about the intricacies of the infield-fly rule ("Now I don't mean to say…"). His voice and volume were at their best out of doors, thundering from a portable radio at the beach or the park, with Allen relishing the way Yogi Berra had just golfed a clutch home run off his shoelaces.

The Dodgers' star broadcaster was also a college man, Walter Lanier (Red) Barber, originally from Mississippi and the University of Florida. Recruited from Cincinnati in 1939, Barber was a master of the southern oral tradition, using wonderful phrases like "the Catbird's Seat" (a poker phrase indicating a prime position) or "rhubarb" (an argument on the field.) Barber, a lay preacher, was far more austere than Allen, declining to root for the Dodgers, and spurning the superstition of not mentioning a no-hitter in progress.

In 1954, Barber moved from the Dodgers to the Yankees. It was bizarre to hear his measured tones emanating from "the big ballpark in the Bronx," as he called Yankee Stadium, but he managed to coexist with Allen, since they alternated three-inning stints between radio and television.

"Brooklyn Against the World"—that says it all.
Courtesy of Brian Strum

Babe Ruth as literary lion; others would follow.
Private collection

Many other fine broadcasters passed through New York. Curt Gowdy worked for the Yankees before moving to Boston and eventually network fame. Ernie Harwell worked for the Dodgers and Giants before becoming a legend in Detroit. Barber's sidekick in

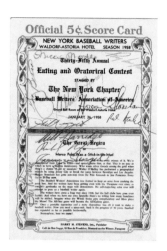

New York Baseball Writers Dinner program, 1958 From the collection of Jerry Stern

Endorsement deals were a big plus to playing in New York Private collection

Brooklyn was Connie Desmond, followed by Vin Scully, out of Fordham University, who would become the voice of the Dodgers in Los Angeles.

The Giants' lead broadcaster was Russ Hodges, with his hearty middle-American sound. Born in 1910 in Dayton, Tennessee, the site of the famous 1925 Scopes trial over the teaching of evolution, Hodges worked for the Cubs, Senators, and Reds before coming to the Yankees after the war. In 1949, he moved across the river to the Giants. He was not nearly as popular as Barber or Allen, but was destined to call perhaps the most famous single play in baseball history.

On October 3, 1951, the Dodgers and Giants played the third and decisive game of their playoff series. With the Dodgers leading 4–2 in the bottom of the ninth, Ralph Branca of the Dodgers came out of the bullpen to pitch to Bobby Thomson.

"Hartung down the line at third, not taking any chances," Hodges announced, for eternity. "Lockman without too big of a lead at second, but he'll be running like the wind if Thomson hits one. Branca throws. There's a long drive. It's gonna be, I believe—the Giants win the pennant! The Giants win the pennant! The Giants win the pennant! The Giants win the pennant! Bobby Thomson hits into the lower deck of the left-field stands! The Giants win the pennant! And they're going crazy! They're going crazy! Oh-ho!"

The various stations did not record the game but Hodges' call was preserved for posterity because a young Giants' fan in the city called home and told his mother to turn on WMCA and push the button on his tape recorder.

There was an ominous sign in the Polo Grounds that day, with only 34,320 fans, barely half the capacity, paying to watch these old rivals play for the pennant. The two owners ultimately decided they could make more money in California, and left after the 1957 season.

The same financial pressures struck the newspaper business. By 1954, the New York daily papers had dropped 9 percent from their 1947 peak while the number of households was growing rapidly. The *Mirror* would close in 1963, and three years later three other papers would merge to form the *World–Journal–Tribune*, known as "the Widget," an impractical hybrid which folded May 5, 1967. The *Long Island Press* went down in 1977. By that time, a new National League team, the Mets, established in 1962, was flourishing in Queens, capturing the loyalties of old Dodgers and Giants fans.

The Yankees dismissed Mel Allen in 1964, after a quarter century of service. He would work on national baseball shows until the Yankees' new owner, George Steinbrenner, welcomed him back into the Yankee family, if not the broadcasting booth. Allen died in 1996 at the age of 83.

Barney [Stein] uses a 4 x 5 Speed Graphic equipped with a 14 inch telephoto lens, and uses Type B Eastman film. The tabloid and syndicate photographers use a 5 x 7 Graflex camera equipped with "Big Bertha" lenses from 28 to 40 inches and 60 inch lenses, giving them a big image.

RED BARBER

Top:
Don Zimmer, 1955
Bowman card
Courtesy of Kevin Bean

Above:
"Daily Mirror"
front page,
October 1, 1951
From the collection of
Jerry Stern

Ralph Branca in straw sennit from Knox the hatter
Courtesy of Brian Strum

Above:
Dizzy Dean, broadcast voice for NBC-TV's Game of the Week
Private collection

Left:
Knothole Gang membership card, with mysterious grommeted disks
Courtesy of Brian Strum

Barber outlasted Allen with the Yankees by two years, being fired for daring to mention the sparse attendance of 413 customers for a makeup game in September 1966, while the Yankees were hitting bottom. He went home to Florida, but staged a renaissance in 1981, joining Bob Edwards every Friday on National Public Radio's "Morning Edition" for a four-minute chat about sports or gardening or whatever he

Clockwise from
Top Left:
Red Barber, here as a Yankees announcer
Private collection

Russ Hodges at the mic
Courtesy of the
National Baseball Hall
of Fame Library,
Cooperstown, N.Y.

Young Mel Allen, up from Alabama
Courtesy of the
National Baseball Hall
of Fame Library,
Cooperstown, N.Y.

Vin Scully in the Dodger booth
Courtesy of the
National Baseball Hall
of Fame Library,
Cooperstown, N.Y.

felt like discussing. At the time of his death in October 1992, Barber was something of a wise old uncle for a large swath of America. Hodges outlasted both his contemporaries as an active broadcaster, moving out to San Francisco with the Giants and dying of a heart attack in 1971, a year after his retirement.

Dick Young became more conservative in his old age, vilifying players who had used drugs and then gone into rehabilitation. "Druggies," he called them. He lamented social and political change in the country he called "My America," and although he criticized the lucrative free agency for players, he left the *Daily News* for the *Post*. He died in 1987, not quite 70.

Having heard my father praise Young when I was a child, I got to work with both of them after my father resumed his career. When I started to cover the Yankees, just out of college, Young would introduce me to players and managers and reporters: "Here's a kid from *Newsday*. He's okay." I figured his personal inconsistencies were his business. Dick Young was an imperfect man but he set a tone for a generation.

WMGM Radio Sport Calendar, June 1949, featuring Marty Glickman
Courtesy of Brian Strum

INNING

5

Ballparks

A Wink and a Smile:
The Real Estate Edge

Andrew Zimbalist

T hese were the glory days indeed—if you were a New Yorker. Between 1947 and 1957 a New York team appeared in a remarkable 10 out of 11 World Series contests. Out of the 11 matchups, a New York team was victorious in nine; seven of those championships were courtesy of the Yankees, with the Giants and Dodgers each chipping in one. Were baseball blessed with perfect competitive balance during this period (i.e., each team having an equal chance of winning), the Yankees, Dodgers, and Giants together would have been expected to win two of the 11 World Series.

With such an un-level playing field, one may have suspected that there were some shenanigans going on in the front office. After all, in this era, baseball's reserve clause was still intact. The reserve clause was a form of indentured servitude for the players that the owners justified to Congress and the courts on the grounds that it provided competitive balance amongst the teams.

But the reserve-clause rationale was always bogus. The New York teams were superior in part because of the size of their market and in part because of, well, front-office shenanigans. The Yankees, alas, were seven times more successful than either the Dodgers or Giants and they all shared the New York market. So what did the Yankees have going for them that neither the Dodgers nor Giants did?

The answer is tied up with the newest element in the baseball business during the glory days—real estate. Team owners began to sell their stadiums and the land they sat on. Once sold, their teams

Ebbets Field turnstile

Courtesy of Gary Cypres, photograph by Susan Einstein, Los Angeles

Aerial view of Ebbets Field

Courtesy of the Barney Stein Collection LLC, photograph by Barney Stein

**Ticket to Washington Park,
predecessor to Ebbets Field**

From the collection of Angela and Thomas Sarro

were no longer tied to their original host city. Now they could move, or at least more credibly threaten to move.

Between the beginning of baseball's modern era in 1903 and 1952, there was a stable roster of 16 teams, each playing in the same city for the entire period. Then, before the 1953 season, Lou Perini moved his Boston Braves to Milwaukee. Next, after Bill Veeck sold his St. Louis Browns, Major League Baseball allowed the Browns to move to Baltimore in 1954. The following year, the Philadelphia Athletics moved to Kansas City. All three franchises had been mismanaged into secondary-team status in their local markets, behind the Red Sox, Cardinals, and Phillies respectively. And all three were distressed economically.

The sale and move of the Athletics opened a new chapter in the business of baseball. Yankees co-owner Del Webb was in the construction business. A Californian high-school dropout, Webb started out as a carpenter but worked his way up. During World War II, his building company landed over $100 million in contracts from the U.S. government, constructing, among other things, military bases and internment camps for the Japanese. Robert Goldwater, Barry's brother, said of Webb: "[He's] an ignorant sonuvabitch who built a million dollars with a hammer and a nail and a case of whisky thoughtfully distributed in Washington."[1]

In 1947, he built the Flamingo Hotel in Las Vegas—the first of that town's luxury gambling hotels—for Bugsy Siegel. Webb's company also took an ownership interest in the hotel, thereby becoming a partner with the notorious operators Meyer Lansky and Gus Greenbaum.[2] Bill Veeck wrote that it was generally understood among the team owners that Commissioner Ford Frick would require Webb to divest himself of his ownership in the hotel as soon as it was financially feasible.[3] Not only did Frick—whose job it was to preserve the integrity of the game—not do this, but he stood idly by as Webb built and became a part owner of another Las Vegas gambling hotel, the Sahara, in August 1961.[4]

After the Braves' first season in Milwaukee proved a smashing success, in December 1953 Webb and Topping sold Yankee Stadium, including its land and adjacent parking lots, plus some minor-league properties, for $6.5 million to a business associate of theirs, Arnold Johnson.[5] A Chicago financier and real-estate speculator, Johnson was a fellow director and owner of the Automatic Canteen Company with Webb and Topping, and also a partner of Webb's in a real-estate project in Phoenix. Shortly after buying Yankee Stadium, Johnson sold the stadium site and the parking lots to the Knights of Columbus for $2.5 million with several buyback options, and then leased the property back for 28 years. He proceeded to sublease the property to the Yankees in a complicated transaction involving options and second mortgages. In the end, Johnson and Webb had worked a deal with handsome tax advantages, potential speculative gains, greater team mobility, and a minimal net-cash investment.

But this was only the beginning of Johnson and Webb's joint machinations in the baseball industry. In 1954 Webb arranged for Johnson to buy the declining Philadelphia Athletics and Shibe Park from the feuding family of Connie Mack. He bought the team and stadium for $3.5 million and then sold the stadium to the Phillies for $1.65 million. Johnson, who had also bought the Yankees' minor league stadium in Kansas City in his purchase of Yankee Stadium a year earlier, then waved the prospect of moving the Athletics to Kansas City before the local pols. The deal was that the team would move if the city bought the local stadium from him for $650,000 and then hired Webb's construction company to refurbish it. In 1955, Johnson's Athletics were playing in Kansas City.

The Johnson/Webb nexus went on to infect the playing field. Between November 1954, when Johnson bought the A's, and the summer of 1957, the Yankees and the A's exchanged 57 players. In his autobiography, Hank Greenberg, former star player and baseball executive, wrote about this relationship between the Kansas City A's and the New York Yankees: "They traded some forty or fifty ballplayers back and forth between the clubs so the Yankees, instead of losing a ballplayer, would trade

Yankee Stadium, "linen" postcard, c. 1950
From the collection of Bob Mayer

Yankee Stadium home plate
Courtesy of Hank Seiden, photograph by David Arky

Ebbets Field Usher Uniform
Courtesy of Gary Cypres, photograph by Susan Einstein, Los Angeles

Ebbets Field
Painting by Andy Jurinko
Courtesy of the artist

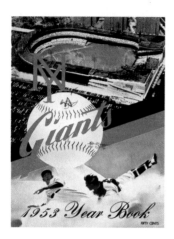

New York Giants 1953 Yearbook
Courtesy of Jerry Liebowitz

Del Webb
Private Collection

**Brooklyn's Washington
Park scorecard, 1900**
From the collection of Angela and Thomas Sarro

him to Kansas City and he'd play there and develop then come back and play for the Yankees again. This, of course, created unfair competition."[6] That is, the A's served as a de facto farm team for the Yankees, enabling the Yankees to get around optioning rules on their players. Through this pipeline passed such Yankee notables as Roger Maris, Ralph Terry, Art Ditmar, and Hector Lopez. Commissioner Frick watched in silence.

As popular as the Dodgers were in Brooklyn, team owner Walter O'Malley was not content playing second fiddle to the Yankees in New York. His park, Ebbets Field, was smaller and inferior to Yankee Stadium in every way. O'Malley wanted the city to provide real estate and infrastructure in Brooklyn to build a new stadium, but he was unable to reach a satisfactory deal with Robert Moses, the New York City Parks Commissioner.[7] To give himself greater leverage and potential mobility, O'Malley took a page from Webb's ownership handbook and sold Ebbets Field.

But nothing seemed to be working in New York, so O'Malley reached a deal with the city of Los Angeles that granted him ownership of 300 acres of land in Chavez Ravine (worth an estimated $18 million in 1957, or the equivalent of $128 million in 2006). The city also agreed to spend some $5 million ($36 million in 2006) providing access roads and other infrastructural improvements.

With the Dodgers' move before the 1958 season, accompanied by Horace Stoneham and the New York Giants who landed in San Francisco,[8] O'Malley not only ended the glory days of New York baseball;[9] he ushered in a new era in baseball economics. The Dodgers had been intensely popular and competitively successful in New York; they were also the most profitable team in the National League. Thus, when they relocated, the Bums became baseball's first franchise not in distress to abandon its host city, setting a new standard for disloyalty.

The soul was ripped out of Brooklyn, but the baseball business had discovered its monopoly power. With only 16 franchises—the same number as in 1903—but a growth in the U.S. population of 2.2 times and in the U.S. real GDP of 5.6 times between 1903 and 1957, there was a tremendous excess demand from U.S. cities to host major league teams. Moreover, since prior to 1955 there were no major league franchises west of St. Louis, half the country was yearning for the national pastime.

Other owners could play the same game as O'Malley. Cities such as Seattle, Denver, Oakland, San Diego, Phoenix, Dallas,

Facing page:
Next to last game at Ebbets; Drysdale pitching, Hodges at third
Private collection

Above:
**Ebbets Field
c. 1920**
Private collection

Right:
**Opening Day at the
relocated home of
the Giants, April
22, 1891**
Courtesy of the National
Baseball Hall of Fame
Library, Cooperstown, N.Y.

Opposite top:
**The Polo Grounds,
a ballpark shaped
like no other, 1944**
Museum of the City of New
York, gift of the Department
of Local Government,
Public Record Office of South
Australia

Opposite bottom:
**Washington
Park, Brooklyn,
Decoration
(Memorial) Day,
1887** Private collection

Clockwise from
top left:

**Yankee Stadium,
September 1948**
Museum of the City of New
York, LOOK Collection,
photograph by Frank
Bauman

**Polo Grounds
scoreboard,
April 1954**
Museum of the City of New
York, LOOK Collection,
photograph by John Vachon

**Hilltop Park, home
to the Highlanders/
Yankees;
Hudson River in
background**
Private collection

**Polo Grounds,
1900, looking at
Coogan's Bluff**
Courtesy of the National
Baseball Hall of Fame
Library, Cooperstown, N.Y.

Left:
**Polo Grounds,
c. 1907**
Private collection

Right:
**Hilltop Park in
Washington
Heights, where
the Yankees first
played**
Private collection

Anaheim, and Minneapolis were more than willing to oblige. At the same time that the baseball barons were learning about their monopoly leverage, however, a concerned U.S. Congress was turning its attention to the sport's judicially conferred antitrust exemption.

Multiple hearings on this exemption were held during the glory years. At one session Commissioner Ford Frick was asked how he felt about baseball's footloose franchises. His answer rationalizes the 1950s moves, but fails to justify subsequent relocations and threats. He told Congress: [10]

There is demand for major league baseball around the country. Now when two clubs or three clubs are in a town and one of them moves, it still leaves that town with baseball. As commissioner of baseball, I think that is good, because you are taking baseball to a new community without leaving the old town barren.

However, when the time comes that you start moving a club from a one-club city to another one-club city merely for the sake of moving, then the commissioner is very definitely opposed....

I think the removal of a club from Washington would be catastrophic. I don't think organized baseball can afford not to be in the nation's capital.

Before he left office in November 1965, however, Frick apparently changed his mind about teams abandoning cities with only one franchise. He watched silently as the Braves packed their bags and moved from Milwaukee to Atlanta. Subsequent commissioners also allowed owners to flex their monopoly muscles.

The glory days in baseball, then, were not only bookmarked by the integration of the game with Jackie Robinson in 1947 and the exodus of the Dodgers and the Giants across the country, but they were also the years when real estate came to the fore. Owners realized that they possessed scarce assets, and that they could leverage this scarcity to gain control over real estate and extract stadium subsidies from American cities. Baseball would never be the same.

Polo Grounds
action, 1905
Private collection

NOTES

1 Quoted in Sullivan, N. 2002. *The Diamond in the Bronx: Yankee Stadium and the Politics of New York.* New York (p. 81).

2. Webb had other real-estate ventures with dubious characters. In 1959, for instance, he bought a 3,000-acre ranch outside Phoenix from a partnership that included Detroit mob boss Joseph Zerilli.

3. Veeck, B. 1959. *Veeck—As in Wreck.* Chicago (p. 246).

4. A fuller treatment of Frick's (and other commissioners') lassitude in governing the game is provided in Zimbalist, A. 2006. *In the Best Interests of Baseball? The Revolutionary Reign of Bud Selig.* New York.

5. Webb and Topping had purchased the Yankees from the Ruppert estate in January 1945 for a reported $2.8 million.

6. Greenberg, H., and I. Berkow. 1989. *Hank Greenberg: The Story of My Life.* New York (p. 215).

7. O'Malley's proposal was for the city to acquire the land at the intersection of Atlantic and Flatbush Avenues (the site of the proposed Nets arena) and sell it to him for $1 million. The initial estimated cost to the city would have been more than $9 million. Later estimates reached considerably higher. O'Malley indicated that he would then put up $4 million of private funds to build the new park. Fetter, H. 2003. *Taking on the Yankees.* New York (p. 220).

8. When approached by O'Malley, Stoneham had been contemplating moving his team to Bloomington, Minnesota. Baseball's insistence on two teams moving together to California and a sweetheart deal from San Francisco (a state-of-the-art stadium built with public money, 10–12,000 parking spaces, and a bargain-basement rent of only $125,000 annually for 35 years) persuaded Stoneham that the West Coast was a better option. He owned the Polo Grounds through September 1961, when it was taken over by the city. The estate of James B. Coogan owned the land beneath the stadium. The Giants had a long-term lease for the land that ran through March 1961. The team paid an annual land rent of $55,000, and also paid all taxes and operating expenses on the stadium. *New York Times*: Oct. 17, 1951, p. 50; Sept. 18, 1963. The Coogan estate and the Giants litigated over the value of the land and stadium with New York; in November 1967 the New York Court of Appeals found in favor of the Coogan estate and the Giants in setting a value for the real estate and plant. During 1962 and 1963, the Mets, after investing $300,000 in refurbishing the facility, rented the Polo Grounds from the city for $6,000 a month (Stew Thornley, personal communication).

9. The enormous impact of the Dodgers' and Giants' flight on New York baseball culture can be sensed by considering that attendance at Yankees games in 1958 was actually lower than it was in 1957—despite the fact that the Yankees competed with two other teams in the local market in 1957 and no teams in 1958. Many former Dodger fans simply abandoned baseball, never to be fans again. It is no coincidence that hundreds of thousands of New York fans turned on to the NFL in 1958, creating an energy that soon spread to the rest of the nation.

10. "Organized Professional Team Sports. Hearings before the Subcommittee on Antitrust and Monopoly of the Committee on the Judiciary, U.S. Senate, 2nd Session, July 1958" (pp. 165, 171).

Ballparks

Ka-ching, Ka-ching: The Real Bottom Line of Baseball in New York

Steven A. Riess

The era of 1947–1957 was the greatest in the history of New York City baseball. In these 11 years, the Dodgers or Giants were in the World Series eight times, each winning once, while the Yankees appeared nine times, yielding seven World Series crowns. The Dodgers and the Yankees were the dominant, extraordinary teams of their leagues; the Giants had the best player of the period—some would say ever—in Willie Mays. The Dodgers and Yankees were the most profitable teams in baseball in this era. In 1947–1956, a period in which the teams submitted financial figures in connection with Congressional antitrust hearings, the Yankees made $3,651,358, or $405,706 a year, just edging out the Dodgers ($3,557,116).

Yet the era ended with the departure of the two National League teams to greener pastures on the West Coast. And in the fifty years since, many fanciful things have been written about how profits eroded or exploded for the three New York teams, why the Dodgers and Giants left, and how much money there was to be made from a baseball franchise in that era, and how. Fortunately, we have some facts at hand.

The owners of all three teams were extremely profit-oriented, unlike the fabulously wealthy Tom Yawkey of the Boston Red Sox and P.K. Wrigley of the Chicago Cubs. The Giants' owner was Horace Stoneham, a Fordham alumnus who had inherited the team in 1936 following the death of his father Charles C. Stoneham, a politically connected curb-market broker, who had secured the

Facing page:
Mantle makes the catch, 1956 World Series at Yankee Stadium.
Museum of the City of New York, LOOK Collection, photograph by Arnold Newman

Ebbets Field, "linen" postcard, c. 1950
From the collection of Jerry Stern

Ticket to first night game at Ebbets field, Johnny Vander Meer no-hitter, 1938
The Bruce Dorskind Collection, photograph by David Arky

Ebbets Field, Brooklyn, N. Y.

Ebbets Field,
"linen" postcard,
c. 1950.
Courtesy of Brian Strum

Ebbets Field, Brooklyn, N. Y.

team in 1919 from the Brush estate. The Giants were the family's prime source of income.

The Yankees owners in 1947 were Del Webb, Dan Topping, and Larry MacPhail, the new team president. They had bought the team in 1945 from the Jacob Ruppert estate and President Ed Barrow at a bargain price of $2.85 million, since the team was worth $7 million, with the intention of making money. Topping had inherited wealth, Webb was a self-made contracting mogul, and MacPhail had formerly run the Dodgers. In 1947 Webb and Topping bought out MacPhail for $2 million, and thereafter Topping ran the team.

The Dodgers ownership situation was more complicated. Branch Rickey, the man who ran the team, had joined the club in 1943 as president and general manager, replacing MacPhail, who had made the club profitable before enlisting in the military. Rickey was a great executive who had built the St. Louis Cardinals into the best team in the NL because of his excellent skill in evaluating talent and his construction of their lucrative farm system. In 1944, Rickey, John L. Smith (president of Pfizer Chemical Company), and team attorney Walter O'Malley bought a one-fourth share of the team held by the heirs of Edward McKeever, and a year later

Ebbets Field, c. 1956

Courtesy of the National Baseball Hall of Fame Library, Cooperstown, N.Y.

In a 1949 Memorial Day day-night doubleheader, the Dodgers split their games with the Giants.

From the collection of Jerry Stern

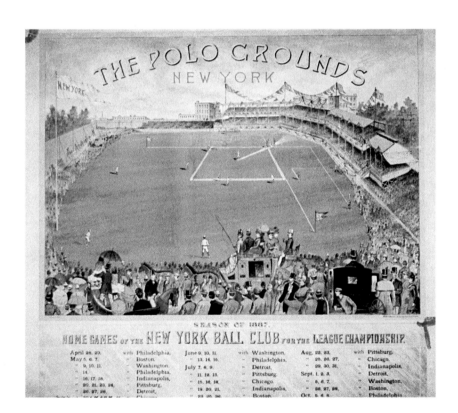

Polo Ground litho with 1887 schedule

Library of Congress

Clockwise From Top Left:
**Action at Hilltop Park,
c. 1910**
Private collection

**Yankee Stadium,
circled by parking lots
and ball fields**
Museum of the City of New York,
Prints and Photographs Collection

**View from outside the
back of Ebbets Field,
c. 1952**
From the collection of Jerry Stern

**Yankee Stadium,
c. 1952**
Courtesy of the National Baseball
Hall of Fame Library,
Cooperstown, N.Y.

Facing Page:
**Fans crowd the Polo
Grounds, 1944.**
Museum of the City of New York,
gift of the Department of Local
Government, Public Record Office
of South Australia

**Sterling silver season
passes and charms,
Polo Grounds**

Courtesy of Millie and Bill Gladstone,
photograph by David Arky

secured the half interest held by the Ebbets family, for a total investment for each of about $350,000.

Major League Baseball prospered after World War II when there was a big pent-up interest in the game and people had a lot of discretionary income to spend on entertainment. New York teams particularly had a great opportunity to make money because of their excellent talent, the city's role as the nation's media capital, and New York's large population (7,891,957 and another 6 million in the suburbs).

The Dodgers were already a big gate attraction, leading the NL in attendance from 1938–43, and in 1945 and 1946 drawing 20 percent of the total NL attendance. Then in 1947, the presence of Jackie Robinson, the exciting pennant race, and a large, loyal fan base combined to generate a franchise-record attendance of 1.8 million. The team fell to third place in 1948 and attendance dropped to 1.4 million. Attendance rose in the pennant-winning 1949 season to 1.6 million, and thereafter wavered between 1 million and 1.3 million at a time when 1 million was a favorable benchmark. From 1946–1952, the Dodgers led the league in attendance five times, and were second in three of the next five years. The team averaged over 18,000 a game, far below Ebbets Field's capacity of 31,902.

The Dodgers benefited from Rickey's massive farm system, comprising about 400 players in 1946, which he used to staff the Dodgers and sell off the surplus. The club made $1,413,325 from player sales in 1945–1948, of which Rickey himself collected 10 percent. In addition, Rickey's base salary was $65,000, plus 10 percent of profits, and a bonus when attendance exceeded 600,000, making him the highest-paid executive in baseball.

The Dodgers were a financial juggernaut, making $2,117,272 between 1946 and 1949, averaging $529,318 a year, with a best of $642,614 in 1949. The team was second only to the Cardinals who averaged $699,072. The club brought in $1.8 million just from home games, compared to the league average of $1.3 million, and $150,000 from media rights—triple the league standard. MacPhail had plowed most of the profits back into the team to retire its heavy debt, but Rickey declared dividends of $173,250 between 1948 and 1950. Despite these profits, and pennants in 1947 and 1949, Rickey did not work well with O'Malley, who pushed him out in 1950, refusing, with the support of Smith's widow, to renew Rickey's contract as president. Rickey than had to sell out to his partners or find an outside buyer. Realtor William Zeckendorf came forward with $1 million, double what O'Malley had anticipated, but he matched the offer.

The Giants fared less well in the 1940s, earning just $290,170, sixth highest in the NL. The team lost money in five seasons, including 1946 when the team

Locker room, Yankee Stadium; Eddie Lopat, June 1954
Museum of the City of New York, LOOK Collection, photography by Robert Lerner and Arthur Rothstein

Yankee Stadium's Grand Opening, April 18, 1923
Courtesy of the National Baseball Hall of Fame Library, Cooperstown, N.Y.

The Polo Grounds and Yankee Stadium were one subway station apart, but people wanted to see the glamorous Yankees.
LEONARD KOPPETT

Yankees locker room,
September 1945;
Manager Joe McCarthy
holding court.
Museum of the City of New York,
LOOK Collection, photograph by
Hy Peskin

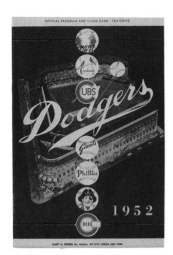

Dodgers program, 1952
From the collection of Angela
and Thomas Sarro

Usher's pin, Ebbets Field
From the collection of Jerry Stern,
photograph by David Arky

came in last. The Giants did have the second-highest gross income in the NL, mainly because of its location in New York, but they also had the second-highest operating expenses. One year later when the team moved up to fourth place, it set a team-record attendance of 1,600,793 and made nearly $530,000, second in the NL to the Cardinals' $630,978. Yet even with that return, the team made just $115,892 from 1946–1949, second lowest in the NL in a highly profitable era. Nonetheless, Stoneham rewarded himself and the other stockholders with $141,012 in dividends—more than the team earned.

The Yankees at this juncture had been for years the most profitable team in the major leagues, and continued to thrive. They led the American League in attendance every year from 1946 through 1959 with the exception of 1948, when they set a club record of 2,373,901. Attendance surpassed 2 million from 1946 through 1950. From 1946–1949, the team made $2,518,885 net. In 1946 the club surpassed $800,000, more than the entire American League had made only one year earlier. In 1947 the Yankees won their first World Series in four years and set a MLB record for earnings with $846,737. In 1946, the Yankees had grossed $3,455,173, $1.3 million more than the Tigers, who came in second in AL earnings. In addition to concessions and gate receipts, the Yankees made around $250,000 from their farm system and about $100,000 from renting their ballparks in New York, Newark, Kansas City, and Norfolk to Negro League teams. The club also made about $45,000 from radio and $75,000 from local television, the first major league team to make money from the new medium.

The general perception in the early 1950s was that Major League Baseball was still prospering. Gross income rose by about a third from $32 million in 1950 to $42.8 million in 1954, and franchises sold for an average of $3.52 million, double the figure of the previous decade. The AL flourished, earning $3,348,043 for the years 1950 and 1952–1956 (there is no data for 1951). However, the NL lost money until the 1955 season.

The Giants, remade by manager Leo Durocher in 1948 into a team that stressed defense and speed, struggled at the box office. The team barely drew one million in 1951 when they won the pennant in one of the most exciting seasons of all time (only 34,320 attended the third game of the playoff when Bobby Thomson's home run won the pennant), as was the case in 1954, when they captured the World Series. Two years later, when the Giants came in sixth, attendance dropped to just 629,179, the lowest in the NL. In 1950 the club lost $264,114, and it lost a total of $286,000 in 1952 and 1953. The Giants bounced back in 1954, making $395,113, second most in the NL, but then just $151,113 in 1955 and $81,415 in 1956. Overall, in the years 1950,

1952–56, the Giants made just $78,488, continuing their financial difficulties from the prior decade—a clear indication of why the team was ready to leave town.

The Giants drew well only when the Dodgers, who produced 34 percent of the gate, were in town. The Giants' woes at the box office could be chalked up to several factors: the team's inconsistent play; the disrepair of the Polo Grounds; the large number of cheap seats; the relatively few expensive box seats; the small number of night games; and the site's declining neighborhood adjacent to Harlem. Stoneham was not heavily reinvesting in his team, which hurt the quality of play, and helped the Giants fall to third in the hearts of New Yorkers.

However, while the Giants were hurting at the box office, their bottom line was bolstered by media revenue. They made $490,192 in 1954 and $730,593 in 1956. The Giants turned a profit in 1956 with the lowest attendance in the league because of the broadcasting money, which comprised 30 percent of their total revenue. They were second only to the Dodgers in media revenue, taking in more than double that of any NL team. Overall, from 1947–1956, the Giants pocketed $405,926, placing them in the top half of the National League, but far behind the other New York teams. President Stoneham himself was not hurting, drawing an annual salary of $70,000, and he put his son on the payroll. In addition, the Giants were one of only two NL teams to pay dividends between 1952 and 1956. These returns surpassed profits, and came at the cost of the team's future.

While the Giants were struggling, their cross-town rivals, the Dodgers, were doing sensationally. The "Boys of Summer" drew at least one million every year, and overall were second in NL attendance. From 1947–1956, the Dodgers made $3,557,115, ($395,235 a year), surpassed only by the Yankees among all major league teams. The team stumbled only in the thrilling 1950 season when the Phillies took the pennant by beating the Dodgers in the last game of the season. The club lost $8,057 that year.

From 1952 through 1956, the team averaged $372,149, a decline from the late 1940s, but the highest in the majors. Nonetheless, O'Malley was not satisfied, and was surely aware of the Braves' move from Boston to Milwaukee; the relocated Braves made twice as much as the Dodgers from 1953 to 1955. But in 1956 the Brooklynites surpassed the Braves ($487,462 to $414,398), following their World Series victory the year before. The Braves outdrew the Dodgers at home, but not on the road. More importantly, the Dodgers made a major league–leading $888,270 from media sources, nearly seven times as much as the Braves.

Walter O'Malley, an unsentimental profit-maximizer, was worried about the team's prospects because his core fan base, the borough's middle class, was bound

Dodgers yearbook, 1953, with Willard Mullin's paranoiac theme
From the collection of Jerry Stern

Dodgers yearbook, 1954, when visions of a new home meant "in Brooklyn."
From the collection of Jerry Stern

Yankees program, 1952

Courtesy of Mike Santo

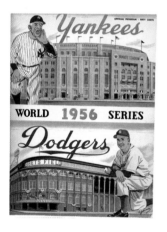

World Series program 1956

Courtesy of Mike Santo

for suburbia. Furthermore, his small park was dated and lacked adequate parking. O'Malley hoped to relocate downtown, but the municipality refused to use eminent domain to help him. So he turned his focus to greener pastures and moved to Los Angeles in 1958, along with the Giants, who moved to San Francisco.

The Yankees dominated the AL off the field as well as on the field, making a whopping 58 percent of AL profits (1950, 1952–1956). The other teams were jealous of the Yankees, but looked forward to their arrival as visitors, since they were a huge box-office attraction. The pinstripers actually fared less well from 1952–1956, when their average profit was $288,868, compared to $603,177 for 1947–1950.

The Yankees typically had the biggest budgets in MLB. In 1946, the team spent $2.1 million, which rose to $3.75 million eight years later. In both cases, the Yankees spent about a third more than any other team in the AL. They historically paid higher salaries—a major segment of team expenses—but from 1952–1956 (except for 1954), the Cleveland Indians outpaid them. The average Yankee salary actually declined from $18,890 in 1952 to $15,830 two years later despite outstanding seasons. Yankee players were actually underpaid because general manager George Weiss was a very difficult negotiator, who considered their annual World Series check part of their regular remuneration. In 1956 the Yankees had the highest payroll in MLB ($492,000), just ahead of the Dodgers ($472,000).

The Yankees' total income rose from $3.5 million in 1946 to $4.2 million in 1950, and to $4.5 million in 1954, of which the biggest chunk was from home games, which brought in $2.5 million in 1950 and leveled off thereafter. Attendance actually fell from 1950 through 1954, when it stabilized at 1.5 million. The biggest growth in income was in radio/television revenues, which rose from $119,935 in 1946 to $675,000 eight years later (double the league average), replacing away games as the second-most important component of revenue. As one wag stated, "It's great to be a Yankee." But it was even better to own the Yankees.

Facing page:
Remember that crazy bullpen location at the Polo Grounds? April 1954

Museum of the City of New York, LOOK Collection, photograph by John Vachon

Stadium seat, Ebbets Field
From the collection of Jerry Stern,
photograph by David Arky

TABLE I. PROFITS FOR NEW YORK MAJOR LEAGUE TEAMS, 1947–1956

	BROOKLYN DODGERS	NEW YORK GIANTS	NEW YORK YANKEES
1947	$519,143	$529,827	$846,737
1948	543,201	(114,286)	516,476
1949	642,614	(88,103)	346,806
1950	(8,587)	(264,114)	497,000
1952	446,102	(222,344)	223,943
1953	290,006	(63,307)	622,185
1954	209,979	395,725	174,876
1955	427,195	151,113	121,852
1956	487,462	81,415	301,483
Total	**$3,557,115**	**$405,926**	**$3,651,358**

Stadium seat, Polo Grounds
From the collection of Jerry Stern,
photograph by David Arky

NOTE. Brooklyn Dodgers profits include associated real-estate companies. Parentheses indicate net loss.

SOURCE: United States, Congress, House Committee on the Judiciary. Subcommittee on Study of Monopoly Power. *Study of Monopoly Power: Hearings before the Subcommittee on Study of Monopoly Power of the Committee on the Judiciary, House of Representatives, Eighty-second Congress, First Session, pt. 6, Organized Baseball* (Washington: GPO, 1952), 1599–1600; United States, Congress, House Committee on the Judiciary. Organized Professional Team Sports. *Hearings before the Antitrust Subcommittee, Subcommittee No. 5, on H.R. 5307 [and Other] Bills to Amend the Antitrust laws to Protect Trade and Commerce Against Unlawful Restraints and Monopolies.* 85th Cong., 2nd sess. (Washington: GPO, 1957), 353.

Stadium seat, Yankee Stadium
Courtesy of Hank Seiden,
photograph by David Arky

Next to last game at Ebbets Field, September 22, 1957; Duke Snider at the bat

Private collection

INNING 6

The World Series

The 1947 Fall Classic and the Rise of Television

Jonathan Eig

There's no way to identify precisely the moment at which baseball became big business. Some say it happened when the Red Sox sold Babe Ruth to the Yankees. Some say it happened when the Dodgers and Giants left New York. Others say it happened when ballplayers unionized. But if I had to pick a moment, I would go with October 2, 1947, when a 22-man television crew fanned out across Yankee Stadium brought World Series baseball to the biggest audience that had ever seen bat meet ball. At that moment, art and commerce collided. Baseball discovered a partner. The hot dog found its bun.

One year earlier, in 1946, NBC had established the first crude television network, linking stations in New York City, Washington, D.C., Philadelphia, and, of course, Schenectady. Now, with the start of the World Series, the network was ready for its first big test.

Though hardly anyone owned a television set, broadcasters nevertheless boldly estimated that 3.9 million people would see the first televised broadcast of the World Series. Most fans would watch the games in a tavern or in front of a hardware-store window or in the living room of some pioneering neighbor who had invested a sizable chunk of his annual income to be the first on his block to own one of the new contraptions. The industry was counting on the Series to introduce the wonders of the new medium and to boost demand. "Winston Television Guarantees: A Front Row Seat at the World Series...with the new 1947

Mantle rounds third, with Crosetti waving him past Robinson; 1956 World Series

Museum of the City of New York, LOOK Collection, photograph by Arnold Newman

You know, we played the Dodgers in a lot of World Series. We thought we were enemies. We weren't. When we're on the field we are, but off the field we weren't. Because I went barnstorming with Pee Wee Reese, Duke Snider and all them guys. And we had fun. But once the games start, you know, you're on your own.

YOGI BERRA

1949 World Series Scorecard

Courtesy of Brian Strum

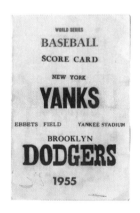

1955 World Series scorecard

From the collection of Jerry Stern

Two second basemen: Billy Martin shows Jackie Robinson how he made the game-saving catch in the 1952 World Series.

Courtesy of the Barney Stein Photo Collection LLC, photograph by Barney Stein

DuMont Teleset," read one big newspaper ad. It worked, too. A decade later, TV sets were in 50 percent of American homes and the World Series was seen coast-to-coast by tens of millions.

Even without TV, the '47 World Series would have been among history's most memorable. It matched the pioneering rookie Jackie Robinson and his upstart Dodgers against Joe DiMaggio and the mighty Yankees. On paper and on the diamond it looked like a mismatch. Brooklyn had no great sluggers and only one imposing pitcher, the 21-year-old Ralph Branca. How they intended to compete with the Yankees, no one

Between 3:44 and 4:01 pm, parents, children, friends and lovers exchanged screams, shouts and expression of joy. Trading on the New York Stock Exchange virtually came to a halt. The phone company later estimated it had put through the largest volume of calls since VJ day a decade earlier. We emerged from the subway into a crowd of hundreds, then thousands of people dancing in the streets to the music of a small band that had occupied the steps of the Williamsburg Bank. Bunting and banners flew from the windows, pinstriped effigies of Yankee players hung from the lamposts, confetti sifted down onto the sidewalks. The traffic was at a complete standstill, but no one seemed to mind. Finding his bus trapped at an intersection, a bus driver abandoned his vehicle and joined the revelers on the street. This night, Brooklyn, not Manhattan, was the center of the world. DORIS KEARNS GOODWIN

Baseball Register, 1955
Courtesy of "The Sporting News"

Don Newcombe, in Game 1 of the 1955 World Series
Courtesy of The "SPORT" Collection

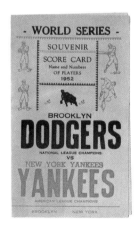

1952 World Series Scorecard
Courtesy of Brian Strum

Johnny Podres cap from Game 7, 1955 World Series

Courtesy of Gary Cypres, photograph by Susan Einstein, Los Angeles

The 1932 Yankees of Ruth and the called shot

Private collection, photograph by Cosmo-Sileo

[Winning the World Series] was something we dreamed about as kids. I dreamed of playing in the World Series against the Yankees.... I wasn't a Dodgers fan until the 1941 World Series, when the Yanks beat the Dodgers. I watched Pete Reiser, and little did I know that one day I'd take his place in center field and play in the World Series with the Dodgers.

DUKE SNIDER

knew. Yet Brooklyn's strategy began to emerge not long after fans settled into their seats and the television cameras clicked on. In the top of the first inning, with one out and none on, Robinson stepped to the plate.

For fans watching on television, it was difficult at times to tell who was who. Shadows falling across the Yankee Stadium infield played havoc with the images on their screens. Eddie Stanky, Pete Reiser, Spider Jorgensen, Pee Wee Reese, and Dixie Walker were nearly indistinguishable but for the numbers on their backs. Yet everyone recognized Robinson, who drew a walk from pitcher Spec Shea, hustled to first, and started dancing off the base. There were three cameras perched on the mezzanine level that day: one focused on the pitcher, one on the batter, and one on the baserunner. All season long, Robinson had been baseball's biggest story. Fans all over the country drove great distances to see him. Over the course of one spring and summer, as he traveled from ballpark to ballpark, he had pushed white Americans to challenge their long-held biases, inspired millions of black Americans to fight for equal rights, and offered a blueprint for the nation's integration. Now he had an even bigger stage. In the top of the first inning, as he took his big lead, threatening to steal, Robinson may have been watched more widely and carefully than any man in the history of the planet.

With little delay, he broke for second. Yogi Berra's throw came in low and late. The Yankees were paying attention now. Everyone was. Two innings later, Robinson drew another walk. This time,

Hank Bauer, who hit in 17 consecutive World Series games, still the record

Courtesy of The "SPORT" Collection

The two MVPs of 1957, in the World Series, 1958 Topps card

Courtesy of Kevin Bean

"Baseball's Fightingest Club," the 1949 Yankees

Private collection

1949 Yankees World Series Ring, GM George Weiss

Courtesy of Ron Leff

1955 Dodgers World Series Ring

Courtesy of Ron Leff

1957 Yankees World Series Ring, Bill Skowron

Courtesy of Ron Leff

The champion Giants of 1954

Private collection

Catch a falling star and put in your pocket, indeed; 1955 Dodger yearbook.

From the collection of Jerry Stern

The 1955 Dodgers

Private collection

Dodgers yearbook, 1952

From the collection of Jerry Stern

The 1956 Dodgers

Private collection

Dodger yearbook, 1956

From the collection of Jerry Stern

I must select this Series [1947] as the most exciting that I know anything about. The involvements of MacPhail, Rickey, Durocher, Shotton and Harris set it up. Jackie Robinson giving his marvelous base-running exhibition as the first Negro to play in a Series ... no Dodger starting pitcher lasting past the fifth inning, and Hugh Casey relieving ... the Bill Bevens-Harry Lavagetto climax in game four ... Joe DiMaggio hitting a home run off Barney ... Allie Reynolds and Frank Shea pitching steadily, and in the seventh game Joe Page turning in the winning job ... the catch by Al Gionfriddo against DiMaggio in the Sunday game. Finally, as the winning Yankees stormed happily into their clubhouse, MacPhail announced he was retiring as president of the club. RED BARBER

Spec Shea was so unnerved that he balked Robinson to second. Black fans at home and in front of their televisions were delirious. White fans were mesmerized. The message could not have been any clearer: That wasn't just a ballplayer running pigeon-toed round the bases; that was democracy in action.

Bill Henry of the *Los Angeles Times* watched on television in the nation's capital, and in his account of the game he sounded at times like a blind man recently given the gift of sight. He delighted at Robinson's "hithering and thithering." He thrilled at the sight of fans in the grandstand grabbing at foul balls. He marveled at the image of the once-mighty Babe Ruth, now a spectator, withered and stooped, heading for the exit as the game's end neared and shadows swallowed the ballpark. "As for the game," he wrote, "it was swell, particularly when you slouched down in your favorite armchair to watch it."

The Yankees took a two-games-to-none lead in the Series. *Finis for the Dodgers*, chimed the headline on Red Smith's column the next day. Had the Series been a rout, television might have scored but a modest victory in its march toward cultural domination. But Brooklyn's Bums were far from *finis*. In Game 3, the Dodgers built a 9–8 lead and called on reliever Hugh Casey to protect it. Casey must have been replaying in his mind that critical moment in the 1941 Series, when his curveball (or his spitball, as some have claimed) struck out Tommy Henrich but got past catcher Mickey Owen. The game should have been over. Instead, Henrich was safe at first, the Yankees rallied for the win, and the Dodgers watched their championship hopes fizzle. This time, though, the reliever managed to put down the Yankee threat. There would be no sweep.

In Game 4, pitcher Bill Bevens of the Yanks, his shirt soaked with sweat, was one out away from a no-hit victory when up stepped one of the more unthreatening hitters in the game, the seldom used

1947 World Series pennant
From the collection of Jerry Stern,
photograph by David Arky

The hobo prince, 1955
From the collection of Jerry Stern,
photograph by David Arky

1951 Yankees World Series Ring, Eddie Lopat
Courtesy of Mike Santo

Sandy Amoros, who made the game-saving catch in Game 7, 1955 World Series
Courtesy of The "SPORT" Collection

Johnny Podres, whose Game 7
shutout in 1955 brought the
Dodgers their only championship
Private collection

Mickey Mantle throws the ball toward thrid
in a World Series game at Ebbets Field.
Private collection

World Series program, Yankees
vs. Giants, 1951
Courtesy of Mike Santo

Cookie Lavagetto. Two men were on base, courtesy of walks, which Bevens had been handing out freely all day (ten in all). The Yankees led by only a run. Lavagetto got a fastball and swung late. To those watching on television it appeared he had his eyes closed upon contact. When he looked up, he saw the ball ricocheting off the wall in right. Both runners came around to score. The Yanks had been one out away from a commanding lead in the Series. Bevens had been one out away from immortality. Now, with only one hit, the Dodgers had won the game and tied the Series.

"MIRACLE" STRIKES FLATBUSH, declared the Brooklyn *Eagle*, for it was newspapers that still mattered most when it came to disseminating news of the game's outcome.

There were no miracles the next day, as the Yankees won easily to go back on top, three games to two. But in the sixth game, the underdogs worked their magic again. This time, the unlikely hero was Brooklyn's Al Gionfriddo, who was playing left field when DiMaggio belted one high and deep into the gap, near the door to the Dodger bullpen. It looked like extra bases, maybe even a homer, when Gionfriddo—sprinting, spinning, stabbing at the air—stuck out a glove and snared the ball just in time. For decades, it would be recalled as the greatest catch in World Series history.

In truth, it was not much of a play. Gionfriddo misjudged it all the way and was surprised and delighted to find the ball in his palm. The catch was remembered as a glorious one largely thanks to television. One camera caught Gionfriddo spinning

Bucky Harris managed the
Yanks to a title in 1947.
Private collection

and lunging and another caught the usually stoic DiMaggio, his head down, kicking at the dirt in frustration. There was no instant replay, yet Gionfriddo's catch nonetheless taught a lesson: No matter how small the screen—and 20 inches by 15 inches was about as big as they got at the time—television had the power to magnify memories. Had he made the play in 1946, all but a relative handful of baseball fans would have relied upon newspaper accounts for a description. In 1947, millions saw it with their own eyes and would never forget.

The Yankees won Game 7, in a fairly uneventful contest. Dodger fans vowed once more that they would wait till next year. But in 1947, the future had already arrived. In one wondrous season, the game had been integrated, televised, and commercialized like never before. A few years later, stations would begin experimenting with color broadcasts of baseball games. By 1951, the national pastime would go coast-to-coast, just in time for viewers to see Bobby Thomson belt a Branca pitch over the wall in left to give the Giants the pennant. The so-called "Shot Heard 'Round the World" was really the "Shot Seen 'Round the World." At the end of the 1957 season, Gillette agreed to sponsor the World Series for five years at $3 million a year, a price that had been unfathomable a decade earlier.

No one at the time seemed worried about how such an infusion of cash would affect the game. Baseball changes and yet it never changes. Fans know this. Baseball is the gasp of the crowd, bodies rising in unison, and a hundred thousand eyes following the ball's arc into the night sky. After 1947 it would also be the sight of a white ball framed by a zooming camera's lens, the expression of an outfielder looking up in despair, and a man with a microphone shouting, *That ball is looong gone!*

It works both ways.

Knuckleballer Hoyt Wilhelm, here with the Giants in 1954
Private collection

One-time Yankee Lew Burdette won three games against his old club in the 1957 World Series.
Private collection

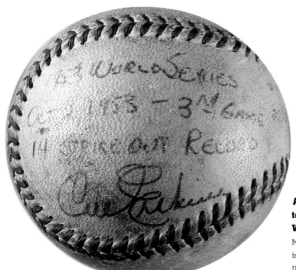

A ball that Carl Erskine used to strike out 14 batters, a new World Series record, 1953.
Museum of the City of New York, long-term loan from State Senator Edward Ford, photograph by David Arky

People talk about that catch and, I've said this many times, that I've made better catches than that many times in regular season. But of course in my time, you didn't have a lot of television during the regular season. A lot of people didn't see me do a lot of things.
WILLIE MAYS

Great Games and Moments

Thomson at the Ferry

Kevin Baker

The best part of any story is what comes afterwards. For me, the defining moment of New York's golden age of baseball came just *after* Bobby Thomson hit his home run to win the deciding game of the 1951 National League pennant playoff between the New York Giants and the Brooklyn Dodgers.

Everyone, or at least anyone who follows the game, knows about the home run itself. "The Shot Heard 'Round the World," the line drive that Thomson smacked into the left-field grandstand on an 0–1 pitch from Ralph Branca. Still the single most famous home run ever struck, bringing the Giants all the way back from three runs down in the bottom of the ninth inning, a feat that had never been accomplished in any of the 360 postseason games played in the history of all major leagues to that point—and which, in the 900 postseason games played since, has never been duplicated. Even after a third-string Giants catcher claimed, decades later, that his own team had been stealing signs, the feat remained undiminished.

But you know all that. You know, too, about the tumult that ensued the moment the ball went into the seats. You have seen the film of Thomson skylarking around the bases, while Jackie Robinson glared at his every step, refusing to leave the field until he made sure that Thomson had touched each bag. You've watched—time and again—Eddie Stanky rushing out of the dugout to jump on Leo Durocher in the third-base coach's box. The two foulest-mouthed, most merciless bench jockeys in the game, the personifications of hard-nosed baseball, cartwheeling down the line together like little

Facing page:
Thomson scoring, Branca walking, Robinson watching.
Transcendental Graphics

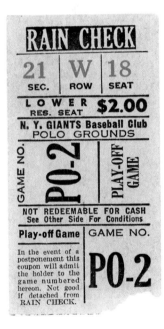

Ticket to Game 3 of the 1951 play-off, the second at the Polo Grounds, and we know how that came out.
Courtesy of Mike Santo

Clockwise from top left:
1957 Yankees program
Courtesy of Peter Knobler

Don Larsen and Casey Stengel, 1958 Topps card
Courtesy of Kevin Bean

Baseball Register, 1951
Courtesy of "The Sporting News"

boys. Thomson literally carried off the field by his teammates as the crowd swarmed around them.

You have heard Russ Hodges' immortal reiteration from the broadcast booth, "The Giants win the pennant! The Giants win the pennant!" (starting that winter, the words were summoned to sell everything from cigarettes to razor blades to baseball cards). You've seen the newspaper photo of Branca crying, stretched out on the club-house steps. You know all the stories, faithfully gathered by countless journalists and historians down the years, of where everyone was and what they did, of smashed television sets and hurled objects, dances of jubilation and fits of despair. (My father, a Giants fan, packing to move to Hollywood and begin an acting career, jumped right over a barrel, a celebration my mother never forgot.) You've read Don DeLillo's speculation on what happened to the *ball* that Thomson hit in "Pafko at the Wall," his unforgettable opening chapter of *Underworld*.

You've been through it all. The high moment of the high noon of New York's greatest baseball era, when all three teams in the city finished first, and it seemed that anything was possible. What could have been more glorious, more perfect? And yet, the chronic writer's question persists: *And then what happened?*

Facing page,
Clockwise from Top:
Mickey and the Duke Courtesy of the Barney Stein Photo Collection LLC, photograph by Barney Stein

Hank Bauer and Joe DiMaggio, September 1950
Museum of the City of New York, LOOK Collection, photograph by Frank Bauman

Ralph Branca in the clubhouse after the climactic game, 1951 Courtesy of the Barney Stein Photo Collection LLC, photograph by Barney Stein

Hank Bauer, 1951 Bowman card
Courtesy of Kevin Bean

After all, some
unexpected things
happen in baseball.
In the ninth inning
of the World Series
game when Lavagetto
got the only hit and
ruined Bevens' no-
hitter, he hit into right
field, the only time
he hit into right field
all season.

GARTH GARREAU

What happens when you've just done something impossible, something no one else has ever done before? It's easy enough to imagine—if unfathomably hard to endure—what Branca, the losing pitcher, went through. Because human existence bends ineluctably to the tragic, we've all had those moments of crushing disappointment, in love, in work; if only in the long, slow grind of life, that moment when we realized that things were not going to work out the way we had hoped they would.

But what happens when they do? What happens when the great, waking daydream actually comes true? What did *Bobby Thomson* do?

He went home. After the obligatory champagne romp, and the press interviews. After he was called out on the top step of the Giants' center-field clubhouse for a raucous curtain call before thousands of adoring, grasping fans still in the stands and massed on the field below; after stopping down at 52nd Street, to sing a Chesterfield cigarettes jingle on Perry Como's TV show for $1,000—more money than any ballplayer of the day could resist—Bobby Thomson went back to the home he shared with his widowed mother on Staten Island.

Usually he took the subway down to the ferry, but this evening he treated himself to a cab down the West Side Highway. Then he paid his nickel like anyone else, and sat unnoticed and alone on the ferry's upper deck, for the 23-minute ride (matching the number on his Giants jersey) across New York Harbor. Once over in Staten Island, he went with his brother—again unrecognized—to meet their mother at a tavern in New Dorp. A crowd of friends and neighbors was already gathered there, and Thomson indulged in a plate of steak and fries and a glass of wine, and was home before eleven o'clock.

Now, I have no idea where Derek Jeter went after the Yankees won their last World Series, but I can tell you for sure that it wasn't New Dorp. I often think of Thomson's circuitous journey home to the city's outermost borough. His time in the cab; walking and riding through the familiar streets of his neighborhood. Above all, I think about his long, quiet trip across the harbor; for those 23 minutes just one more commuter, getting back late from the office. It is impossible to imagine any star departing so quietly after such a moment today, and it seems to me the very essence of the urban experience, the chance to be both in the world and apart from it, anonymous in the crowd.

In this sense, Thomson's trip home is also emblematic of what was most endearing about New York's golden age of baseball; that is, how the game was held in perspective.

It might be said that there have always been two New Yorks. One of them is the Big City, "the Empire City of the West." The

Facing page,
Top to Bottom:
**Yankees Exhibit
card, 1950**
Courtesy of Kevin Bean

**Yankees Exhibit
card, 1951**
Courtesy of Kevin Bean

**Yankees Exhibit
card, 1952**
Courtesy of Kevin Bean

**Larsen in action
during perfect game**
Museum of the City of
New York, LOOK Collection,
photograph by
Arnold Newman

Ralph Branca, 1949
Bowman card
Courtesy of Kevin Bean

world capital of finance; the nation's largest city and its first capital. The home of its major media headquarters, its publishing industry; its fashion, advertising, theater, art; its trendsetters and its beautiful people, its hipsters and hypesters. The other New York, of course, is the Little City, the New York of countless, individual neighborhoods—so many that one can live in the city for decades without ever setting foot in some of them. Here are the homes of its working people, who keep the physical city running. People of every possible ethnicity, race, religion; their neighborhoods tied together by so many intricate, often invisible customs and rituals, some of them stretching back for generations.

Above:
In the Yankee dugout, no one would talk to Larsen during the game.
Museum of the City of New York, LOOK Collection, photograph by Arnold Newman

These two New Yorks, Big City and Little City, have existed simultaneously for centuries, one overlaid on the other like a map transparency. They are aware of each other, they interact with each other, but it is entirely possible to live in one New York without paying any attention to the other. Nevertheless, their fortunes are wholly interdependent, and the best moments in New York's history have always come when both cities are flourishing.

Facing page:
Larsen flanked by Mantle and Bauer for postgame interviews.
Museum of the City of New York, LOOK Collection, photograph by Arnold Newman

In the years after World War II, Big City and Little City reached a rare equilibrium. New York had never been more exciting, had never struck a more prominent figure on the world stage with the competition—the great capitals of Europe and Asia—still

Johnny Podres, 1957
Topps card
Courtesy of Kevin Bean

> I was so cocky at
> that particular time
> when I was young,
> whatever went in
> the air I felt that I
> could catch. That's
> how sure I would
> be about myself.
>
> WILLIE MAYS

Top right:
**Mantle leads off first,
but the vendors make
the picture, Game 5,
1956 World Series.**
Museum of the City of New York,
LOOK Collection, photograph by
Arnold Newman

Above:
**Mantle leads off first,
Maglie checks him and
Hodges holds;
Game 5, 1956 World
Series.** Museum of the City
of New York, LOOK Collection,
photograph by Arnold Newman

freezing, or digging out of the postwar rubble. It was now the most populous city in the world, and the unofficial world capital, with the United Nations having alighted on the shores of Turtle Bay. Its writers, its artists, its theater, and its popular culture had all become preeminent, even dominant; it was more than ever the central ganglia of business and finance around the globe.

But most of all, New York in the first twenty years after the war was a great middle-class town, in a way that it had never been before, and never will be again. For the first time in almost two decades, millions of families in the city had some disposable income, and something to dispose it on. For the first time in over a century, or ever since their ancestors had first come ashore at Castle Garden, many of them had a good chance to rise up from the working class into which they had been born. The union wages they now earned were augmented by a network of social welfare that provided cheap public housing; cheap and efficient public transportation; neighborhood pools and recreation centers; even a free, first-rate, education up at City College.

The entertainment was better still. For a very reasonable fee, a middle- or working-class resident of the city could catch a Broadway show during what was also the golden age of the American theater. They could still go stompin' at the Savoy, or see the best jazz that was ever played up at Small's Paradise in Harlem, or in the Latin

Facing Page,
Clockwise from
top left:
**Ralph Branca
Exhibit card, 1948**
Courtesy of Kevin Bean

**Bobby Thomson
Exhibit card, 1949**
Courtesy of Kevin Bean

**Don Larsen
Exhibit card, 1957**
Courtesy of Kevin Bean

**Willie Mays
Exhibit Card, 1952**
Courtesy of Kevin Bean

Ralph Branca

Bobby Thomson

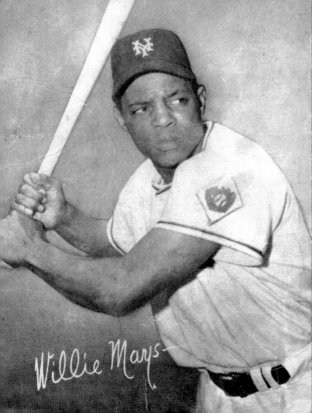

Willie Mays

Don Larsen

The Giants won Game 1 The Dodgers won Game 2 when Clem Labine hurled a 10-0 shutout. Newcombe had the start for Game 3 and took a three-run lead into the ninth inning. [One run scored and] two "seeing eye" base hits brought the potential winning run to home plate in the person of Bobby Thomson. Charlie Dressen called the bullpen at the Polo Grounds, where Branca and I were warming up. Clyde Sukeforth answered the phone. "They're both ready," he said. "However, Erskine is bouncing his overhand curve." Dressen said, "Let me have Branca." On Ralph's second pitch, Thomson hit a three-run homer to win the game and the pennant. Whenever I'm asked what my best pitch was, I say, "The curveball I bounced in the Polo Grounds bullpen." CARL ERSKINE

So much heartbreak contained herein: "Phantom" World Series press pin, 1951. Courtesy of Alan Zucker, photograph by Michele Zucker

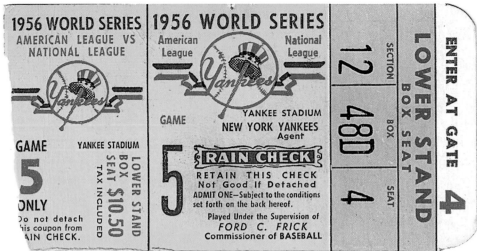

Above:

**Official scoresheet,
Larsen's perfect game**

Courtesy of the National
Baseball Hall of Fame Library,
Cooperstown, N.Y.

Top right:

**Ticket to Game 5 of the
1956 World Series**

Courtesy of Alan Schwarz

Quarter clubs along 52nd Street, or down in the Village. They could while away the summer days out at Coney Island, on the beach or in the glass emporium of Luna Park. Or they could go see three of the most memorable ball teams that ever played the game.

Which was a privilege they frequently neglected. The other, pertinent fact about that final playoff game between the Giants and the Dodgers—after Thomson's home run, and his long journey home—is the attendance. It was 34,320, or just over 60 percent of the Polo Grounds' capacity. This has been attributed to rumors that the game was sold out, but the meager crowd was not an aberration. Baseball games rarely sold out in the great age of New York baseball. All three teams had set attendance records in the years immediately after the war, but their gates had declined repeatedly thereafter. In 2006 the Mets alone—only the second-most-popular team in New York that year—would outdraw all three of these legendary ball clubs *combined*, in the last year they were in the city together.

Some have attributed this to the dry rot beneath the glimmering façade of the Big City. To the galloping deindustrialization of New York, or the deteriorating neighborhoods, and the depredations of Robert Moses; to the small but steady increases in crime in the neighborhoods surrounding Ebbets Field and especially the Polo Grounds; the white (and then black) flight that had already begun to afflict the city. Yet none of this changes the fact that in 1951 most New Yorkers had more money than they had ever had before, or that they followed baseball avidly in the city's eight dailies, on the radio and the new television channels. With the proliferation of night games and weekend doubleheaders, with 22 games a year

**The Yankee
Stadium scoreboard
at the faitful
moment**

Courtesy of the National
Baseball Hall of Fame
Library, Cooperstown, N.Y.

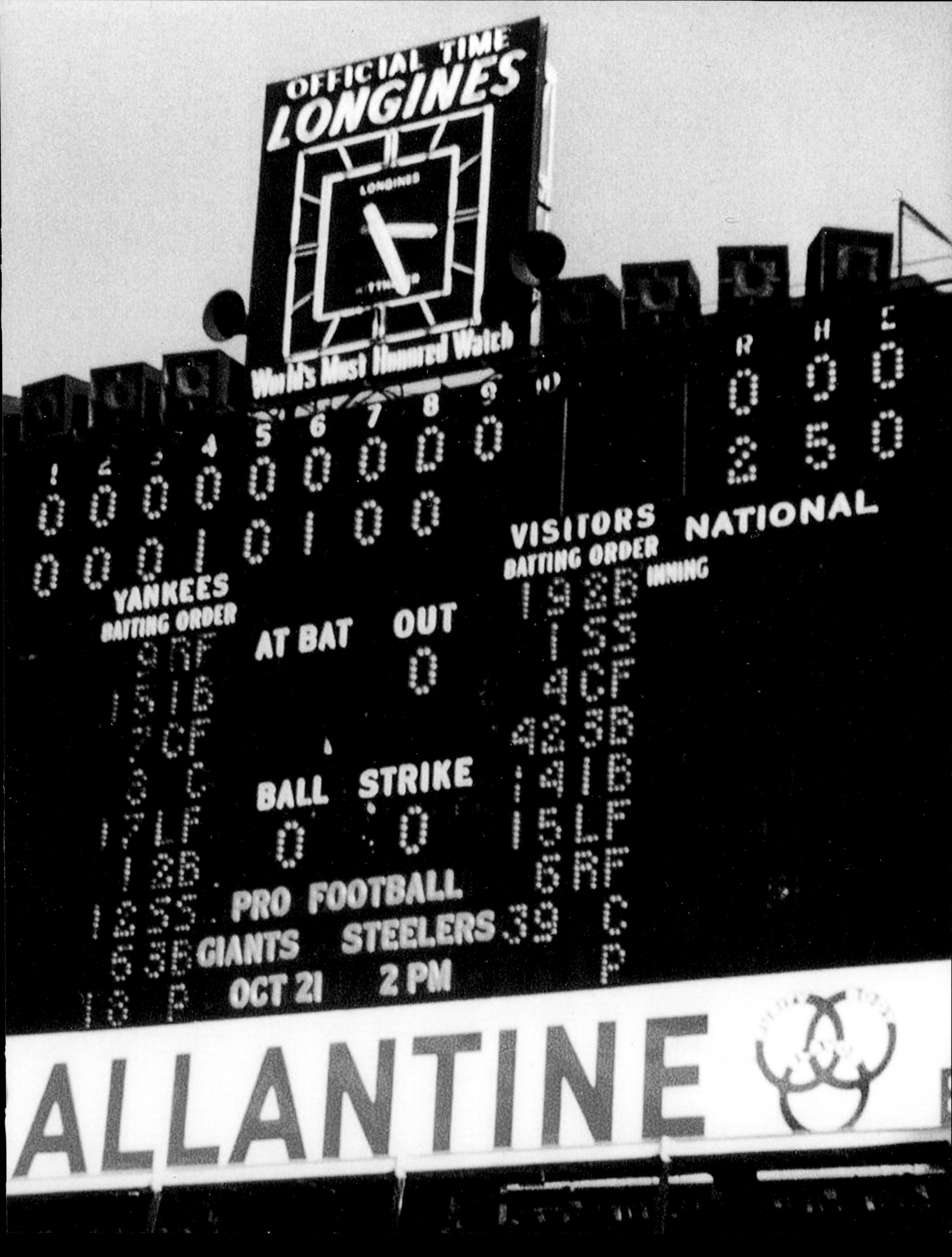

OFFICIAL TIME
LONGINES

World's Most Honored Watch

R   H   E
0   0   0
2   5   0

VISITORS   NATIONAL
BATTING ORDER   INNING

1 9 2B
1 5 SS
4 CF
4 2 3B
1 4 1B
1 5 LF
6 RF
C
39 C
P

YANKEES
BATTING ORDER

9 RF
15 1B
7 CF
6 C
7 LF
1 3B
12 SS
6 3B
18 P

AT BAT   OUT
0

BALL   STRIKE
0   0

PRO FOOTBALL
GIANTS   STEELERS
OCT 21   2 PM

BALLANTINE

Don Larsen's 97th and final pitch of the game, October 8, 1956

Private collection

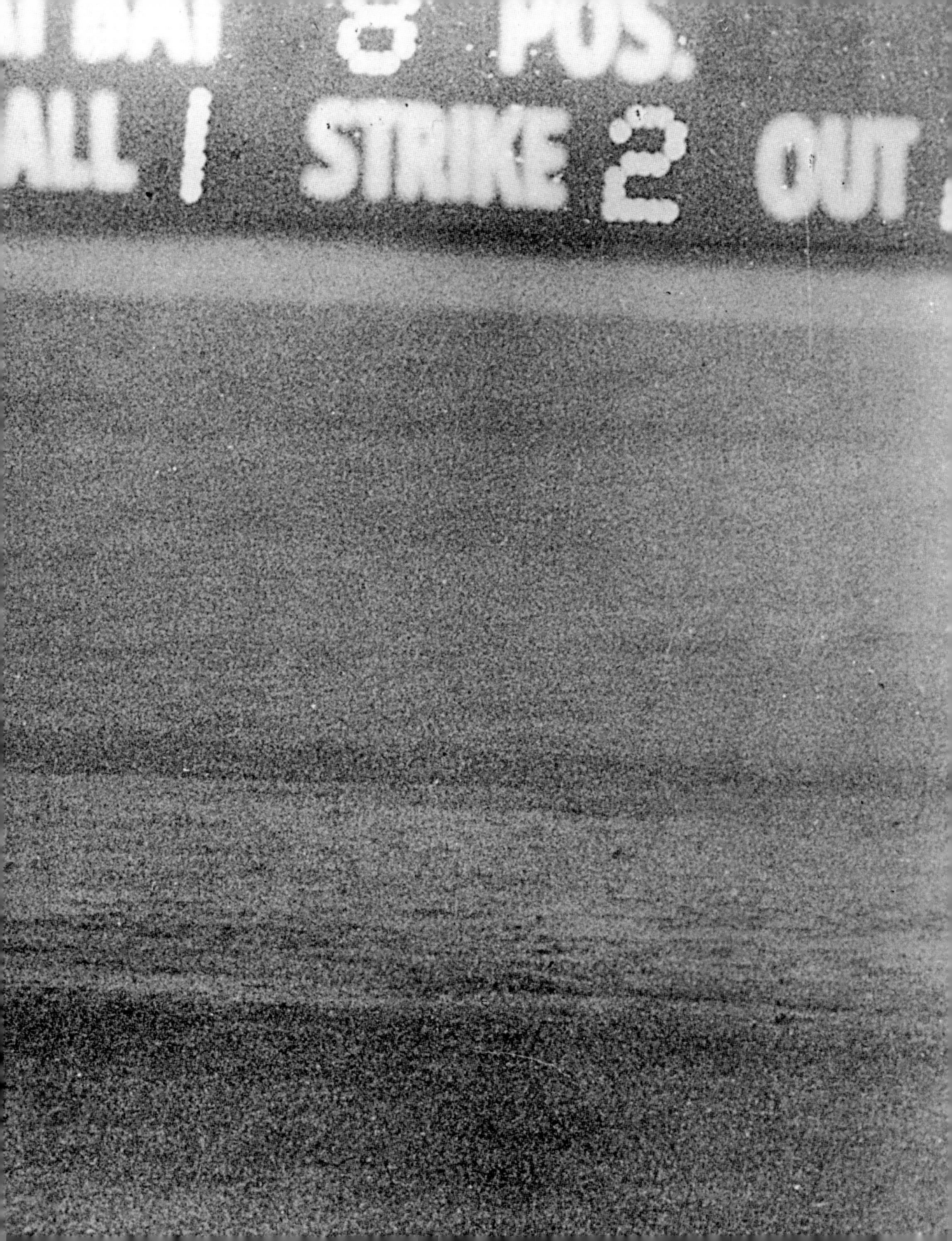
8 POS.
ALL 1 STRIKE 2 OUT

Johnny Antonelli, 1954 Topps card
Courtesy of Kevin Bean

A despondent Branca
Courtesy of the Barney Stein Photo Collection LLC,
photograph by Barney Stein

I think about it every day. Sometimes it's hard to believe it ever happened. I'm glad it did because everybody thinks about that and forgets all the mistakes I made in my career.

DON LARSEN

between those two bitter rivals, the Dodgers and the Giants, attendance should have been skyrocketing.

Why wasn't it? The best answer I can come up with is that people had other things to do on a weekday afternoon in the fall of 1951. They had work or school to go to, chores to perform around the house, social obligations to attend to. In short, they had lives—and lives that were not fixed in orbit around the doings of celebrities. In that era before the velvet rope and the VIP room, baseball players—even stars—were surprisingly accessible. Regular people could gain entry to legendary watering holes such as 21 and Toots Shor's, the Stork Club and El Morocco. One of the most famous off-the-field incidents of the time, the brawl at the Copacabana in 1957 that got Billy Martin traded out of town, started when Martin and several of his Yankee teammates confronted a bowling team that had been heckling Sammy Davis Jr. A *bowling* team! It is, again, hard to picture Derek Jeter getting into an altercation with any such plebeians.

Most players already made more money than schoolteachers, or cops, or firemen—but not a lot more. Fans honored them with "days" for which they chipped in and bought their favorite players sets of dishes, or stoves, or refrigerators (or, in

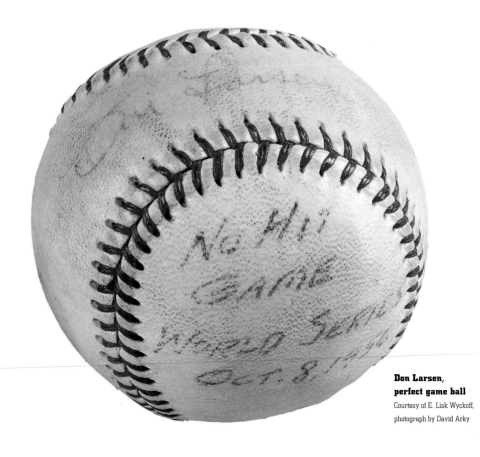

Don Larsen, perfect game ball
Courtesy of E. Lisk Wyckoff,
photograph by David Arky

Berra meets Larsen for postgame bearhug, Game 5, 1956 World Series
Museum of the City of New York, LOOK Collection, photograph by Arnold Newman

one instance, a cow), and the players were glad to get them. They worked regular jobs in the off-season. Ralph Branca was a haberdasher and an insurance agent, while Mickey Mantle went back down into the mines his father had worked during the first few years of his professional career. They often lived right in the neighborhood. Duke Snider, Pee Wee Reese, and Carl Erskine all resided on middle-class blocks in Bay Ridge, while Jackie Robinson became the first black man to integrate not only the National League but also Snyder Avenue, in East Flatbush. Many of the Giants lived on the Upper West Side during the summer, or up in Harlem itself, where Willie Mays famously played stickball in the streets with the local kids. The Yankees often spent the season in motels along the Grand Concourse, even well into the 1960s. Mantle and Roger Maris shared an apartment in Queens the year they both chased Babe Ruth's record, and even when Mantle was residing intemperately at the St. Moritz Hotel in 1956, he often used to walk to Yankee Stadium through Central Park.

It must have been exciting to know that the gods lived among us, just as in ancient days the old pagan deities must have inspired all the more awe, seeing as how you might catch a glimpse of one romping through the woods—or perhaps loping along in the shadows at the edge of the Great Lawn. These were the days when the crowd could still be trusted to leave the park by walking across the field at the end of the game. Both fans and players headed for home the same way, with a sense of themselves and their place in the world that kept the game in balance; hoping for just a few minutes' grace on the subway or the ferry or the bus, when they might look back with quiet satisfaction on a good day and a job well done. This was New York.

Believe it or not, Wink [Bobby Thomson's girlfriend and future wife] wasn't there when I hit the home run. She worked in the social services department of a New Jersey hospital and couldn't get off that day. The interns at the hospital knew she and I were dating so they invited her up the back stairs to the interns' quarters, where they listened to the game on a tiny transistor radio. When things looked so bleak in the ninth inning, Wink promised all the interns champagne if the Giants pulled the game out. She figured she was pretty safe, but didn't complain later when she had to pay them off.

BOBBY THOMSON

Great Players and Managers
Forever Mick

Jane Leavy

"Snider, Mantle, Mays. You could get a fat lip in any saloon in town by starting an argument as to which was best."—Red Smith, *New York Herald Tribune*, 1954

Some arguments are meant to be fought, not won. In the gilded Fifties, when center field was the center of sport, and New York was the capital of baseball, Duke Snider, Mickey Mantle, and Willie Mays divided boroughs and housing projects, families and siblings, street corners and schoolyards. In a 1994 monologue for Ken Burns' PBS baseball series, Billy Crystal distilled the essence of the debate:

> "…Willie's unbelievable! Willie's the greatest. He can do anything!"
> "You're nuts. The Duke, the Duke is a classic. See how he runs with his elbows up like that?"
> "You guys are nuts. It's Mickey and that's it. He's strong. He's blond. He's blue-eyed. He hits from both sides with power. I think you guys should reconsider."

Of course, Billy was a Mickey guy. Or: Mickey was his guy. Whichever linguistic formulation you chose, the relationship was proprietary and said something about who you were. If trying on mother's spike heels was one way to practice how to be a woman, then arguing the merits of Willie, Mickey, and the Duke was a methodology for trying on manhood.

Facing page:
Mantle had more power from the right side of the plate. Private collection

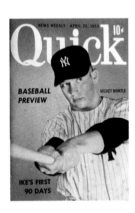

Mickey Mantle, "Quick," April 20, 1953
Transcendental Graphics

Babe Ruth's key fob
Courtesy of Hank Seiden, photograph by David Arky

It was easy to want to be Willie. He was so blithe. As the renowned baseball expert Tallulah Bankhead once said: "There have been two geniuses, Willie Mays and Willie Shakespeare." Who wouldn't want to try on the accoutrements of incandescence?

Duke had his partisans too. He lost the National League batting championship to Mays on the last day of the 1954 season. The Duke of Flatbush, not the Say Hey Kid and not the Commerce Comet, led all major league batters in home runs and RBIs in the Fifties. He was the perfect overlooked, underdog emblem for an overlooked, underdog borough and an overlooked, underdog kid.

Mantle's life story had the quality of a libretto, full of grand themes and passions ending in tragedy. Far more than Mays and Snider, he fit the classical definition of a hero. He had more injuries than Achilles—and showed up for work every day for 18 years.

Mantle required imagination: not just the elastic capacity to envision the vanishing point of all those home runs interrupted by Yankee Stadium's iconic infrastructure, but the imagination to conceive how far he would have gone unimpeded by injury—the prodigious *what if.* "There's a kind of Greek mythology tragedy thing about him," said Frank Martin, a Pennsylvania welder who took a day off from work to videotape his funeral. "He has never been what he should have been. He was a very human hero."

To assume his limp—or his twang, as Billy Crystal did for his Bar Mitzvah speech—was to practice how to function with disappointment and disability. Mantle did it with honesty. When I asked him back in 1983 to compare himself to Mays, he shook his head and muttered, "Fuckin' Willie."

Then he began to sing Terry Cashman's nostalgic anthem, "Talkin' Baseball," but he forgot what came after the refrain: *Willie, Mickey and the Duke.* "I know all the words to 'I Love Mickey,'" he assured me. "Teresa Brewer wrote it. *I love Mickey. Mickey who? The fellow with the celebrated swing.*"

Eleven years after his death, Mantle is far more of a celebrity, far more of a public presence than either of his surviving compatriots. The confluence of disposable income and baby-boomer sentiment transformed him from a has-been into an economic juggernaut. Universally regarded as the father of the modern age of sports memorabilia, Mantle saw the value of his 1952 Topps baseball card soar; today it sells for as much as $275,000.

In December 2003 the Mantle family held an auction at Madison Square Garden. The big-ticket items made headlines: $41,300 for the 535th home-run ball; $198,000 for the 1956 Sultan of Swat crown; and $275,000 for his 1957 MVP Award trophy.

More staggering were the prices commanded by the contents of his junk drawer. An unemployed limousine driver from Brooklyn

Facing page:
Willie Mays
Museum of the City of
New York, LOOK Collection,
photograph by Earl Theisen

I don't think any city had three [managers] of that stature around at the same time. There was Leo Durocher, my manager on the Giants, he was fiery, outspoken, tough. He also knew baseball strategy inside and out. There was Casey Stengel of the Yankees. He could out-talk, out-platoon, and many times out-think all the competition. There was Walter Alston of the Dodgers, the strong, silent type, he was a man's man and a guy dedicated to the game and to the people of Brooklyn.
MONTE IRVIN

Leo Durocher
Private collection

Mantle with the Joplin Miners in 1950 Private collection

Mantle and Berra, 1957 Topps card
Courtesy of Kevin Bean

I was a lousy catcher 'til they got Bill Dickey there. Dickey worked me hard. I liked it, though. And then it came easy.
YOGI BERRA

paid $649 for three Mayo Clinic appointment cards and $1,888 for a bankbook from the First State Bank of Commerce, Oklahoma, which was a lot more than Mickey ever had in the account.

In such a world is it any wonder that the Hall of Fame expressed serious interest in acquiring a full set of Mantle's toenail clippings for its permanent collection? The exchange of letters between Ted L. Nancy and Cooperstown was published in *Letters from a Nut*, a book of absurdist correspondence that may or may not have been ghost-written by Jerry Seinfeld, a Mets fan.

Statistics do not explain the devotion. True, Mantle played in more games than any other Yankee at a time when the Yankees were the most televised franchise in the country. True, he played on twelve pennant-winning and seven world-championship teams. He still holds World Series records for home runs (18), RBIs (40), runs (42), walks (43), extra-base hits (26), and total bases (123). In his final World Series in 1964 he had three homers and eight RBIs and batted .333.

True, he was white at a time when the game was on the precipice of true emancipation. African American ballplayers—Mays, Hank Aaron, Jackie and Frank Robinson, and Maury Wills would change the face and style of the game forever.

True, he had one of the greatest offensive seasons ever when he won the Triple Crown in 1956, the only time he completely fulfilled the burden of his potential. But he finished his 18-year career with a batting average below .300. "Every time I'm introduced and someone says, 'He was a lifetime .298 hitter,' I think, 'You cocksucker, quit saying that.'"

No doubt, he would be gratified to learn how well he fares in the latest Sabermetric analysis: His OPS (a combination of slugging average and on-base average) places him 12th all time, far better than Mays (29th) or Snider (47th). In the Win Shares system pioneered by Bill James, which measures how many wins could be attributed to an individual's play, Mantle ranks second only to Babe Ruth.

But none of that explains how or why he morphed into part of the zeitgeist—a reference point for the zeitgeist sitcom, "Seinfeld." When Jerry needs a metaphor for the subterfuge of breast-augmentation surgery, it's like Mickey Mantle corking his bat. When George contemplates parenthood, he vows to name his first-born "Seven."

Peter Mehlman, a reformed sportswriter (and transplanted New Yorker) who wrote those episodes, says:

The image of an All-American hero retired with Mantle. He was the last hero before the onset of anti-heroes—Ali, McEnroe, Dick Allen, John Carlos, Angela Davis, Jane Fonda, Charles Manson, Badass Budinsky, Serpico,

*Lennon, Ellsberg, Butch and Sundance, Joplin, Archie Bunker, Trapper and
Hawkeye, Woodstein.*

*He was the last sports hero we had while we still felt good about ourselves as a
country—before JFK was shot and Vietnam and Watergate all took away our
innocence. He was the last sports hero on the scene at a time when America and the
world seemed to still make sense, the last guy it was still cool to worship before we
all became too jaded/cynical/suspicious to admit we loved anyone. Mantle rose
with the post-war rise of America, peaked at the peak of America and declined
with the decline of America.*

Mantle was the last boy in the last decade ruled by boys. Broad, blond, blue-eyed,
he looked like Dick of "Dick and Jane" all grown up. He looked the way we wanted to
see ourselves. Even in Brooklyn when Joe Torre was growing up there, you had to wear
your hat like Mickey Mantle. A half century later, the Yankee manager demonstrated
the technique: First you rubbed the front of the cap (a B in his day) with spit. Then
you wrapped the brim around a ball and stuck it in a coffee cup on the kitchen table. It
was called "the Mantle Roll" and was as popular in the cornfields of Illinois as it was on
the sidewalks of Brooklyn.

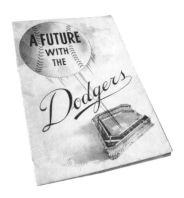

"A Future with the Dodgers" recruitment brochure Courtesy of Brian Strum, photograph by David Arky

Chesterfield advertisement featuring Gil Hodges, c. 1950 Courtesy of Gary Cypres, photograph by Susan Einstein, Los Angeles

Phil Rizzuto and his wife, Cora, February, 1959 Museum of the City of New York, LOOK Collection, photograph by Frank Bauman

With his limitless potential, Mantle was America incarnate. His raw talent was a metaphor for the land's natural resources and for postwar optimism. His tensile strength—wrought not from weight machines and steroid injections—was a by-product of actual work. The obtruding veins in his neck and arms evoked the veins of ore that miners like his father pulled from the earth.

Ordinary baseball language couldn't contain him. The tape-measure home run was invented to describe the ball he hit out of Washington's Griffith Stadium in April 1953. Later, Red Patterson, the genius PR man, would admit there was no tape measure. But by then, the hyperbolic formulation had passed into idiom. Mickey had become synonymous with American clout. Poor Chuck Stobbs, the pitcher on the other end of the parabola, won't discuss it. Not even with his wife. "I stick to my business and he sticks to his," she said.

The American dream is inherently subversive, a daring dogma, revolutionary in the assertion that anyone can grow up to become someone in America. Anyone can grow up to be President or Mickey Mantle—even Mickey Mantle. He recognized this. "I could have ended up buried in a hole in the ground and I ended up being Mickey Mantle," he told a business partner later in life. "There must be a god somewhere."

Mantle was Lana Turner waiting to be noticed at Schwab's Soda Fountain. He was the optimistic rebuttal to Brando's plaintive cry—I coulda been a contender. If a strapping boy from Oklahoma whose only other prospects lay below the earth's surface could be unearthed, could soar to his father's imagined heights, then anyone could make it in America. "I guess you could say I'm what this country is all about," Mantle once said.

Weekly now, in an ongoing effort to merchandise and profit from the past, *The New York Times* offers for sale photographs of dead Yankee sluggers. The most haunting of them is a portrait of Mantle walking through empty aisles at Yankee Stadium, glove on hip, looking over his left shoulder for someone or something. The image offers no clue why he's in full uniform, in an empty ballpark, alone. He appears without peer or audience. *He just is.* The vast stadium drapes his shoulders as if resting on them. The picture captures at once his strength and his burden, his omnipotence and his loneliness.

Ultimately he crumbled beneath the weight of expectations imposed by his father, his manager, his fans, and himself. No one human being could shoulder the weight of the American dream.

Conspicuous consumption became his second career. Women, booze, business opportunities, he ran through them all—without exhausting a seemingly infinite reservoir of public goodwill. "If I

Facing page:
Robinson, Hodges, Campy, Cox, Reese
Private collection

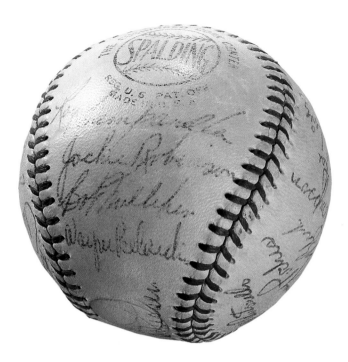

Mantle drag bunting
Private collection

The classic Mays swing, 1954
Museum of the City of New York, LOOK Collection,
photograph by John Vachon

knew I was gonna live this long, I woulda taken better care of myself," the aging Mick liked to say. And it always got a laugh until he died of cancer brought on by cirrhosis of the liver.

If at the beginning he was the incarnation of the strong silent Fifties (surly was the word writers used most often for him because they couldn't write what he actually said), he evolved into a psychobabble raconteur, the Will Rogers of postmodern athletes. He turned effusive, laying himself on the public couch with touching naiveté and reflexive honesty, recounting the particulars of his recurring nightmares for analysis. It is hard to imagine Joe DiMaggio discussing bedwetting with Johnny Carson.

By the time of his death in August 1995 he had evolved into an avatar of the confessional Nineties. He went into rehab, became a 12-step prophet preaching the gospel of recovery and redemption in the pages of *Sports Illustrated*. It was a cautionary tale: the aftermath of the formerly famous. When he faced the cameras for the last time two months before his death, he was a husk of a man, shrunken by cancer, smaller than life. The brim of his 1995 All-Star Game cap dwarfed the now desiccated features. There was no Mantle Roll. "Don't be like me," he said.

A year ago or so, Robert Pinsky, the former poet laureate of the United States, who is no Yankee fan, was in Washington to discuss his book about King David, a man of Biblical contradictions: shepherd, poet, warrior, adulterer. "In some ways, he was a lot like JFK," Pinsky said. "He was one of those guys you liked anyway."

Facing page
(left and right):
**1953 Dodgers
signed ball**
Courtesy of Brian Strum,
photograph by David Arky

**Ball signed by
Larry, not yet
Yogi, Berra.**
Courtesy of E. Lisk Wyckoff,
photograph by David Arky

Right:
**Wille Mays and
Giants on the bus,
1954**
Museum of the City of
New York, LOOK Collection,
photograph by John Vachon

Bottom, left:
**Carl Erskine,
1956 Topps card**
Courtesy of Kevin Bean

Bottom, right:
Yogi Bera, 1957
Museum of the City of
New York, LOOK Collection,
photograph by Arnold
Newman

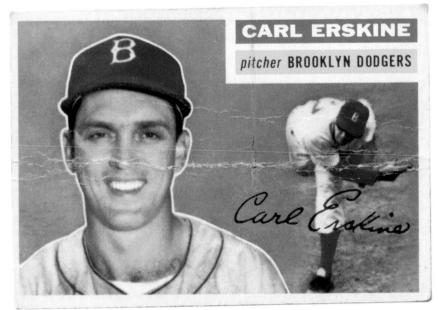

CARL ERSKINE
pitcher BROOKLYN DODGERS

Mantle triptych
Private collection

I was pitching batting practice when [Mickey Mantle] took his first swings. The kid hit the first six balls nearly five hundred feet, over the lights and out of sight. He hit them over the right-field fence batting right-handed and over the left-field fence batting left-handed. And remember, Mantle was only 18 at the time. I played with Gehrig

and with Ruth and I've seen fellows like Jimmie Foxx and they hit
prodigious home runs in their day but I have to say Mantle hit more
tape-measure home runs consistently than any of those players.
Mantle outdrove them all. BILL DICKEY

Phil Rizzuto, the Scooter
Private collection

**Yankee Locker room, left to right:
Skowron, Rizzuto, Lopat**
Museum of the City of New York, LOOK Collection,
photography by Robert Lerner and Arthur Rothstein

Eddie had another losing day. He just sits there, thinking it over and cooling out. He's always the last one out, and that's why I consider frozen foods the greatest boon the housewife ever knew. I wait till I hear him at the door, and then I start the meal.

LIBBY LOPAT,
wife of Yankee pitcher

The Mick was also one of those guys. Bob Costas alluded to this paradox in his eulogy, calling Mantle "a fragile hero to whom we had an emotional attachment so strong and lasting that it defied logic."

We still do and it still does—certainly at the "Heroes in Pinstripes" Fantasy Camp, a yearly pilgrimage to youth held in Ft. Lauderdale, Florida, long under the auspices of Mickey's old teammates, Moose Skowron and the recently departed Hank Bauer, who had poked a gnarly finger in my chest and chirped, "Nothing negative! Nothing negative! *Nothing negative!*"

There under the Florida sun, men of a certain age and certain wealth (this fantasy does not come cheap) donned pinstripes to frolic on the grass where Mantle once roamed. Among them was Paul Berkman, a Manhattan investment company executive whose grandfather was an usher at Yankee Stadium. He worked the box seats near the dugout along the third-base line and parked his grandson in the box nominally reserved for the owner of the visiting team. "I was going to Yankee Stadium before I remember going to Yankee Stadium," Berkman said.

He remembers the first time he saw Mantle up close, reaching out to touch him, the shoulder that seemed too big to be true, just to see if he was real. Then, one day when he was fifteen or so—definitely not drinking age—a beer truck pulled up at the player's gate and the beer distributor said, "Hey, kid, you want to get into the Yankee clubhouse?"

"What kid doesn't want to get into the Yankee clubhouse? He had me carrying beer into the clubhouse. The door to the trainer's room was open. Mickey was lying on the table. The trainers were stretching out and measuring yards upon yards of tape for Mickey. As a kid, the sheer quantity of it was daunting. He had to be put together like a mummy."

Now, fifty years later, with the number 7 draped across his back, Berkman revisits the argument over Willie, Mickey, and the Duke. "People have a tendency to root for the underdog. Wilt Chamberlain once said, 'Nobody roots for Goliath.' Mickey was both. He was Superman and the underdog. There was an underdog quality even when he was the greatest player on the field. Our awe at his accomplishments was exceeded only by our amazement that he could do anything at all."

So, metaphorically anyway, he was David and Goliath. He was that unique combination of godly and oh-so-achingly human; bigger than life and less than the sum of his parts. A young boy—and even some little girls—could aspire to godliness and identify with fallibility. He inspired awe without envy—unless it was for what he got away with, the excess that finally caught up with him.

In the summer of 2006, the U.S. Postal Service released a new set of stamps memorializing the careers of Mel Ott, Hank Greenberg, Roy Campanella, and Mickey Mantle. Lonnie Busch, the designer, had never heard of Ott or Greenberg. Everything he knew about Mantle he learned from watching *61**, Billy Crystal's HBO movie about the race between Mantle and Roger Maris to surpass Babe Ruth.

Busch created an image of the switch-hitter batting right-handed. His arms extend beyond the frame, jutting out of the picture, too big to be contained. His unformed visage gazes beyond the pitcher toward an uncertain future. The green copper frieze of the House that Ruth Built — the ballpark Mantle carried — rests squarely on his shoulders. The crowd recedes and surrounds him.

What exactly was he trying to capture in that sticky, one-by-one-and-a-half-inch rectangle? "The light within the darkness," the artist replied.

Left:
Casey Stengel, 1951 Bowman card
Courtesy of Kevin Bean

Right:
**Mickey Mantle, 1952 Bowman
card—kept for a reason**
Courtesy of Kevin Bean

The End
Farewell to the Polo Grounds
Ray Robinson

The Polo Grounds, that ancient bathtub of a ballpark,
was where:
Matty and McGraw reigned
The Babe prevailed
Ott raised his right leg
Hubbell screwballed
Merkle forgot to touch second
Willie made the Catch
Thomson tore the heart out of Brooklyn
Another Mays killed a batter
Dempsey butchered the Wild Bull of the Pampas
"The Four Horsemen" were born
Durocher buried nice guys

O n the afternoon of July 4, 1939, at Yankee Stadium I was a bleacher celebrant of Iron Horse Lou Gehrig as he said his farewell to baseball.

On the night of July 31, 1940, at the Polo Grounds I saw catcher Hank Danning of the Giants bang a ninth-inning home run off Bucky Walters of Cincinnati, to defeat the Reds 5–4 after they had led 4–1. Willard Hershberger, catching that night for the Reds, was morose after the game. "I called for the wrong pitch," he insisted. Several days later Hershberger's body was found in a hotel bathroom. He had cut his throat with a razor blade.

On the night of August 3, 1979, I attended a game at Yankee Stadium, following the death of Yankee captain and catcher Thurman Munson in a plane crash in Ohio.

In a different way than Jackie Robinson, he stole home: a prize from the Polo Grounds finale, September 29, 1957.
The Stephen Wong Collection

The Polo Grounds wrecking crew dressed for the occasion.
Private collection

Baseball, like some other sports, poses as a sacred institution dedicated to the public good, but it is actually a big, selfish business with a ruthlessness that many big businesses would never think of displaying.

JACKIE ROBINSON

By now it should be abundantly clear that I have had a penchant for sitting in on some of baseball's most melancholy moments, either by design or inadvertence. So it should not be surprising that I was one of 11,606 pallbearers for the New York Giants when they played their final game at the Polo Grounds on September 29, 1957.

My friend Arnold Hano, who had written a gem of a memoir called *A Day in the Bleachers*, celebrating the first game of the 1954 World Series and memorializing Willie Mays' miracle catch, phoned to ask if I'd accompany him to the Giants' last rites. "You can bring along your own crying towel," he suggested.

Ever since Mays joined the Giants in 1951, I had become a fervent Giants fan. Before that I usually had rooted for individual players, going back to Gehrig, southpaw Herb Pennock, Mel Ott, and Blondy Ryan—yes, Blondy Ryan—without actually giving my heart to the teams that they played for. The fact that the Giants were now leaving New York for a West Coast venue was something that I took personally. So did Hano. We had no patience for a world in which the Giants were in San Francisco, a Republican was President, subway fares were going up, newspapers were folding, and black kids were being turned away from school doors in Little Rock by Arkansas governor Orville Faubus.

Giants program and ticket from Opening Day, April 18, 1957, plus yearbook and coaster
Courtesy of Peter Knobler, photograph by David Arky

New York City used to be a manufacturing town. After the war, I got a job putting eyes in dolls at the Imperial Crown doll factory for twenty-two dollars a week. The center of the toy and novelty industry was in New York, and it averaged about twenty-six thousand workers. They tried to blame the unions for manufacturing dying out. It was really the imports.

JULIE ISAACSON,
It Happened in Brooklyn, 1993

Above:
Willie Mays' glove
The Stephen Wong Collection

Below:
Joe DiMaggio's bat from the 1949
All Star Game played at Ebbets Field
The Stephen Wong Collection

Mr. Peter Campbell Brown
Corporation Counsel
Municipal Building, Room 1656
New York 7, New York

Dear Pete:

The town looks brighter. I'm glad you and your bride are back, tanned, taller, broadened and full of culture. I find from personal experience that these manifestations wear off quickly, so we are planning another trip soon and hope you are too.

Apropos of this morning's news grist, I hope you won't give the time of day to Walter O'Malley's latest "offer." The Atlantic Avenue site is dead for a Sports Center. Time, delays and other factors have killed it. Nor will the improvements other than a Stadium work there without housing. Title One is pretty nearly out, which leaves housing to Larry Gerosa under the Mitchell Lama Act and gives him a golden opportunity to demonstrate his theories on clearing sites first and finding sponsors and tenants afterward.

Acquiring land for sale to Water O'Malley is not a public purpose and would be a scandalous procedure anyway. The Authority is out of business and can't finance anything, whatever its original possibilities may have been.

What remains is Flushing Meadow. We could find out in two weeks whether we could get a reliable concessionaire who would pay $400,000 a year rent, the amount needed by the City above parking revenues to amortize a $10,000,000 stadium ready on June 1, 1959.

What Walter says about foundation problems at Flushing Meadow is rubbish. We know every yard of it. No trouble with parking and the open spaces and the building would be on piles.

Let's meet soon.

Best,

Robert Moses [signed]
Co-Ordinator

The Giants of 1957, under their manager Bill Rigney, were a pretty dismal out-fit, despite the presence of the ineffable Mays, Johnny Antonelli, Dusty Rhodes, and the 1951 home-run hero, Bobby Thomson, who had spent the early part of the year in Milwaukee. Their record of 69–85 landed them in sixth place, with an average of only 8,000 people coming to see their home games. It was then that their not-so-sober owner, Horace Charles Stoneham, arranged to take them away from us. Hano would remind me that when Thomson hit his "shot heard 'round the world" against the Dodgers there were some 20,000 empty seats in the Polo Grounds. That was a har-binger of why Stoneham plotted to remove his club from our sight, propelled by the bullying of Dodgers owner Walter O'Malley.

Keep the Dodgers in Brooklyn, a "spontaneous" demonstration.
Courtesy of the National Baseball Hall of Fame Library, Cooperstown, N.Y.

The shutout was very subtle. Nobody said where you could and couldn't live, but where a bank might give a black person a mortgage on Hancock Street, it would never give him a mortgage in Bay Ridge. White people could move wherever they wanted to and as redlining and blockbusting started to happen, they got out of the neighborhoods.

WILLIAM THOMPSON,
It Happened in Brooklyn, 1993

The loyal and substantial fan was replaced by the undesirables. I brand no race, color, or creed as objectionable. They all have their scum. But unfortunately, the scum was now thick in Brooklyn.... In our Ebbets Field location we were close to 400,000 people within walking distance, in addition to two subway lines, bus lines, and half a dozen trolley car lines feeding us—yet they would continue to supply us with the same element of people, a pretty indigestible potpourri.... Manufacturing companies move ... perhaps to a state where they get a tax break, raw material is handier, shipping costs less. Why not a baseball team? In a nation of free enterprise, is it wrong to wish to improve yourself? FRESCO THOMPSON, O'MALLEY'S AIDE

Above:
Unused ticket to the last game at Ebbets Field, Dodgers 2, Pirates 0
The Bruce Dorskind Collection, photograph by David Arky

Right:
Singing into the wind: "Lets Keep the Dodgers in Brooklyn" sheet music, Famous Music Co., 1957
Courtesy of Gary Cypres, photograph by Susan Einstein, Los Angeles

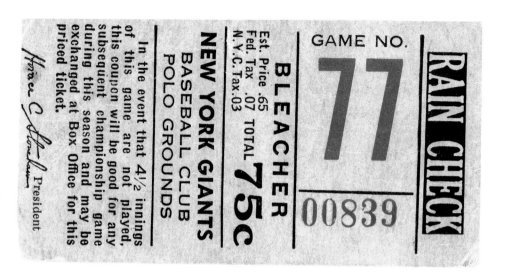

The writer's ticket to the last game at the Polo Grounds
Courtesy of Ray Robinson

"I think it's our duty to say goodbye to these guys," Hano said to me. So we journeyed to the Polo Grounds ("a terrible place to watch a ball game," baseball historian Robert Creamer once wrote), where we bought seats — 75 cents, including tax — in the splintery bleachers. That was exactly where Hano had positioned himself for Willie's catch three years earlier. The bleachers accommodated about 3,900 people. It seemed to me that about half of these seats were occupied for this valedictory.

As we settled into our seats that overcast day I asked Hano if he thought that any of our fellow bleacherites had seen Bobby's home run, or Willie's catch. Or if they had been present for any of Master Melvin's blasts over the nearby right-field wall.

"These are diehards," he replied. "They have been Giants fans for a long time." I noticed that there were no vendors selling hot dogs. But Ballantine's Beer was available at a single concessions stand, despite the "Have a Knick" advertising that confronted us. As the game went along, with Arnold diligently tending to his scorecard (I refused to join in the exercise, making a political statement), the fans became alternately scornful and sarcastic. One wise guy near us drew some laughs when he growled, "If the Giants don't win, nobody will show up tomorrow." Another bedraggled fellow, who appeared to be in his eighties, wielded a homemade banner imploring the Giants to stay. Others expressed their contempt for Stoneham in scatological fashion. A clever detractor shouted, "We ought to stone him!" Still another voice asked, "Where the hell is San Francisco?" The fans were much livelier in every sense than the players, who appeared to be walking through their roles. The flags atop the ballpark hung limply against their poles. Nobody seemed to care about the ultimate result of this finale under Coogan's Bluff. For the record, the score was Pittsburgh 9, Giants 1.

The Goldschmidts were the first to move. As more families migrated to the suburbs each year, automobile sales continued to grow. Though they were sad to leave, the lure of more bedrooms and larger rooms proved irresistible. Television, once a source of community, had become an isolating force.
DORIS KEARNS GOODWIN

Above:
Last banner to fly over Ebbets Field
Courtesy of Gary Cypres, photograph by
Susan Einstein, Los Angeles

Right:
**September 24, a date that will
live in infamy.** Courtesy of Gary Cypres,
photograph by Susan Einstein, Los Angeles

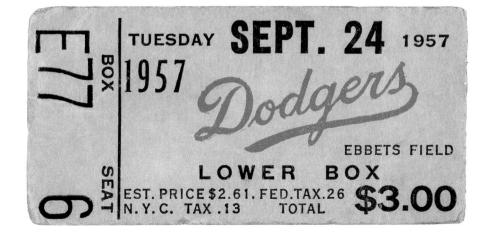

When I went behind
the bat in the windup
game in Ebbets
Field, I knew it was
goodbye to that cozy
park. It was Thursday,
September 28, 1957
[actually it was
Tuesday, September
24] and the few fans
on hand for the wake
waved goodbye after
the final out.
ROY CAMPANELLA

**Off to the Hollywood Boulevard
of broken dreams.** Courtesy of Gary Cypres,
photograph by Susan Einstein, Los Angeles

Hand-colored song slide depicting Polo Grounds crowd, c. 1910
Private collection

Two Friends Award, given to Pee Wee Reese and Jackie Robinson in 1956 by Atlanta's "100 Percent Wrong Club." The Stephen Wong Collection

When the Dodgers left, the feeling died. It wasn't just a franchise shift. It was a total destruction of a culture.

JOE FLAHERTY

"This game," said Arnold, "is the saddest thing I've ever seen." On a couple of occasions, right fielder Don Mueller of the Giants played balls poorly. But the official scorer failed to charge him with errors. "I guess the scorer fell asleep," said someone sitting near us. However, when Giants catcher Wes Westrum, a notoriously poor hitter, came to bat he was greeted with wild applause. And even though Mays failed to get a hit that afternoon, he unleashed one of his typical muscular throws, throwing out a Pirate runner who was trying to stretch a triple into a home run. Thomson bungled a play at third base and seemed to laugh so hard at his misdeed that his shoulders shook. At that moment the fans laughed along with the gentle Bobby. Even the gaunt Rigney, Durocher's successor as Giants pilot, received a polite round of applause when he stuck his head out of the dugout. It was that kind of a day—wretched baseball, nastiness at times, grumpy gratitude.

When Willie stepped into the Polo Grounds batter's box for his last time, the crowd cheered heartily. After he grounded out the crowd cheered again. It reminded me that when I went to see Babe Ruth as a little boy, fans would roar approval, even as he lashed the air for a strikeout.

The game ended as Rhodes, once the unlikely hero of the 1954 World Series against Cleveland, grounded out feebly to shortstop. Hano, ever the griot, pointed out that the man waiting on deck was Thomson, the icon of '51.

It was over. But not for the fans.

Immediately the Giants players, fearful that their uniforms would be ripped off their bodies, left the dugout, and fled towards the clubhouse in center field. I'll never forget the sight of the heavy-legged Rhodes beating Willie to the stairs, proving what an unbalanced diet could do for a fellow. A voice then came over the loudspeaker asking departing fans, now in a restless and rebellious mood, not to come on the field. Such injunctions were scarcely heeded; most of the fans were in no mood to be told what to do.

Within a few minutes, the field was crowded with souvenir-collectors—scavengers would be the politest way to describe them. Like a bunch of unleashed ants, these marauders went about tearing large plots of grass out of the diamond, ripping the bases loose from their moorings, uprooting home plate, snatching the bullpen telephones and stealing advertising signs. Another group massed in front of the club-house windows, raising their voices in a dispiriting song:

> *We hate to see you go,*
> *We hate to see you go,*
> *We hope to hell you never come back,*
> *We hate to see you go.*

"The Wide Swing," Harvey Dinnerstein's painting of Joe DiMaggio at the 1949 All-Star Game in Brooklyn; see the bat on page 188. The Stephen Wong Collection

Ebbets Field, view from the left-field roof, 1955
Courtesy of Sports Legends and World Heroes, photograph by Hy Peskin

This simple celluloid pinback said, "Freedom."
The Stephen Wong Collection

Ticket to Opening Day at the Los Angeles Coliseum, April 18, 1958 and invitation to groundbreaking for Dodger Stadium at Chavez Ravine, September 17, 1959
The Bruce Dorskind Collection, photograph by David Arky

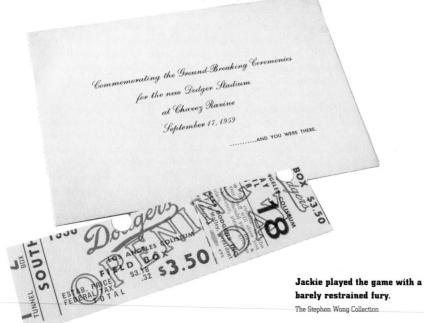

Commemorating the Ground-Breaking Ceremonies
for the new Dodger Stadium
at Chavez Ravine
September 17, 1959

...........AND YOU WERE THERE.

Jackie played the game with a barely restrained fury.
The Stephen Wong Collection

Willie Mays' cap, 1954

The Stephen Wong Collection

Three dimensional cardboard display of the World Champion Dodgers in three rows, issued by Schaefer Beer Co.

The Stephen Wong Collection

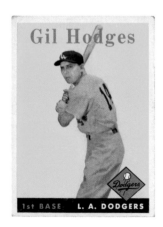

Gil Hodges, 1958 Topps card... with the Dodgers of Los Angeles

Courtesy of Kevin Bean

Hano and I fully expected that the dugouts, where once the spikes of Matty, McGraw, Hubbell, Ott, Hughie Critz, Monte Irvin, Al Dark, JoJo Moore, Hal Schumacher, Freddy Lindstrom, Travis Jackson, and so many other National League immortals had left their imprint, would also be carted off.

That didn't happen. But the thought occurred to us that Hano should have hauled off the bleacher plank that he sat on the day Willie made his catch.

Looking back at that anarchic scene, I recalled reading how voyeuristic aficio-nados of the ill-starred, 31-year-old matinee idol Rudolph Valentino went berserk at his funeral in midtown Manhattan during the Roaring Twenties. And I remembered, too, how ghouls searched the site of the plane crash that killed Notre Dame's football coach Knute Rockne in Bazaar, Kansas, in 1931. Rockne's rosary and other belongings disappeared, much as the Polo Grounds appurtenances did 26 years later.

As we rode home on the subway that 1957 day, Hano and I swore that we would never again give our hearts or our ticket money to another baseball team. But it wasn't long before both of us, disenchanted as we were, tuned in to the San Francisco Giants games in the wee hours of the morning. We were pleased to listen to Les Keiter's artful reconstructions of Giants games taking place 3,000 miles from the Polo Grounds.

After all, we still had Willie Mays to root for, even though he was now in a faraway place where people booed him and cheered Nikita Khrushchev.

Home plate from the Giants' last game, with four tickets from the fateful 77th home game of that season, plus autographs— including that of old Hans Lobert, a Giant from 1915-17.

The Stephen Wong Collection

EXTRA INNING

What Came Next
The Legacy
Alan Schwarz

They were 13 years old then. That makes them about 23 now, old enough to have wafted off and even had kids of their own, starting the cycle anew. But on the morning I spent with them 10 years ago, they were still in one classroom, sitting at their desks — strangely eager — sixth graders at a very special school on one very special day.

On April 15, 1997, I took the 4 train to Crown Heights and PS 375, a.k.a. the Jackie Robinson Middle School. This wasn't just any other morning. Later that night, at Shea Stadium in Queens, the New York Mets, Major League Baseball, and even President Clinton would be honoring the 50th anniversary of Robinson breaking baseball's modern color barrier by suiting up and playing for the Brooklyn Dodgers. We would, and did, hear the full spectrum of testimonials to Robinson's "drive" and "courage" and "importance" — well rehearsed platitudes, scripted and worn, all out of the mouths of fiftysomethings for whom Jackie Robinson's legacy was long ago fired into iconographic permanence. Far more interesting, I suspected, would be to watch the Robinson legend germinate in the minds of the young, to witness how the next generation took the baton. So I went to the middle school—named after Robinson himself—that sits across McKeever Street from where once stood Ebbets Field. I wasn't disappointed.

"Even though he's gone we still have a piece of him inside all of us, that tells us anything we want to do and we put our minds to it we can do it no matter what other people say," Judah Ragin wrote in his essay. A few chairs away, Brendan Smith's Fila sneakers fiddled nervously under his desk as he wrote; he knew he wasn't getting every word right, but he knew what he was feeling: "Sometimes people say and do things to me. They say I can't do anything. I start to feel very bad … but before I start I stop and thing about Jackie Robinson and what he did inspired me."

Facing page:
Gone but not forgotten
Courtesy of the Barney Stein Photo Collection LLC, photograph by Barney Stein

The pennant domination by the three New York teams—principally the Yankees, of course—made the national pastime a rather parochial pleasure; it was hard for fans in Pittsburgh or Detroit to wax rhapsodic over a Subway Series. No, the blessings of the 1950s were not unmitigated, any more than on the national scene the tranquility of the Eisenhower years were without cost.
JOHN THORN

1986 celluloid pins, world champion Mets

Courtesy of Andy Fogel

Jackie Robinson has reached the rarest echelon of heroism in America: one that is organic. His significance is not inert, allegorical fact, like "Paul Revere" or "Neil Armstrong," a first-black-ballplayer factoid passed from one generation to the next like a set of old cufflinks. No. Robinson's story is not of one size or shape but, like clouds, becomes what the onlooker sees in it. Underdogs plan. Targets stiffen. Outsiders dream. Jackie Robinson has become what people need from him.

Even children. And thank goodness, because many young people—even folks in their thirties—are having increasing difficulty believing that the world Jackie Robinson conquered ever existed. It's simply unfathomable today to imagine Michael Jordan, traveling with his new wife to training camp, getting kicked off a flight, being refused service at a coffee shop, have WHITES ONLY signs sneer at him atop restrooms and drinking fountains, have to get off another flight when a white couple strode on board, and then settle for a 32-hour bus ride (in the last row, naturally). For all the progress yet to be made, this world has vanished—and so quickly that most American History programs, which rush-rush-rush before summer just to get through World War II, have yet to figure out how to deliver real texture to our neighboring era, just beyond the fence of shame.

Not so in Brooklyn that morning, though. In some ways the kids did the teaching. The young New Yorkers assembled by class and marched around the four blocks that once ensconced old Ebbets Field, now a drab housing development but the spot where Jackie Robinson changed their world forever. They started on McKeever, parallel to the old third-base line, the first kids in each group carrying a banner. "Thank You, Jackie," one read. Another: "Class 606, The Next Jackie Robinsons." It was to be a silent march, and the hour-long ceremony was about as silent as junior-high kids ever get. Passersby watched with curious smiles. Cops redirecting traffic clapped.

Press pin for the 1960 World Series portraying Yankees manager Stengel, fired after the club's defeat. Originally owned by Mr. Christie Bohnsack, Museum of the City of New York, gift of Olga Lewando, photograph by David Arky

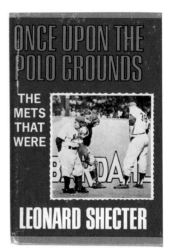

"Can't anybody here play this game?" Casey used to wail about his Mets. Private collection

In a strange twist, the architect of the move, Walter O'Malley, was (and in the East, still is) widely seen as the snake in baseball's version of the Garden of Eden, responsible for ending the grand old game's paradisical age. Yet the placement of franchises in California, as distressing as it was for Brooklyn and Manhattan and as roundly condemned as it was by traditionalists, may now be seen as the best thing to happen to baseball in the decade. And Walter O'Malley, if you will permit your mind a considerable stretch, may be viewed not as the snake offering baseball the mortal apple but as a latter-day Johnny Appleseed (in the footsteps of Alexander Cartwright, who in 1849 also headed for California in pursuit of gold, yet who is remembered not for his venality but for bringing the New York Game to the West). JOHN THORN

Clem Labine "was kind of a cocky, arrogant type, which was good. I liked it," said Dodgers and Mets teammate Roger Craig.

Private collection

A lot of people didn't know the man for what he was. He stood by me every minute after my accident, helping me to see my way through. No one knows that after that wonderful night he had for me in the Coliseum when 93,000 showed up, he gave me a check for $50,000. And he continued my salary, which was more than $50,000 a year, for years after that. He was a great pioneer in integrating baseball. He was the attorney and part owner of the Brooklyn Dodgers when Jackie Robinson, Dan Bankhead, Don Newcombe and Roy Campanella were signed. If we had more people like Walter O'Malley, this world would be a much better place.

ROY CAMPANELLA

Program, luggage tag and ticket from the Dodgers goodwill tour of Japan in 1956, in which they played exhibitions against that country's major leaguers, were seeds for growth and change.

From the collection of Jerry Stern

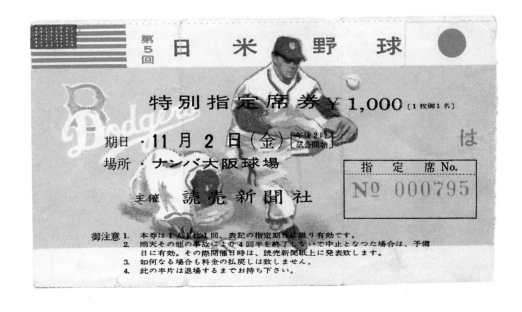

Big Newk did not fare well in Los Angeles.

Private collection.

After a dismal first year in Los Angeles, the Dodgers won a World Series in 1959.

Private collection

WILLIAM A. SHEA

In New York, disgusted baseball fans and civic leaders first reacted to the loss of National League ball by trying to hijack another Senior Circuit team.

In December 1957, New York Mayor Robert F. Wagner, up for reelection, appointed a four-man committee consisting of former Postmaster General James Farley, department store king Bernard Gimbel, real estate executive Clint Blume and high-powered attorney William A. Shea to engage a new team.

Shea would become the key figure in this drama. Born in New York on June 21, 1907, Shea grew up on a steady diet of baseball, attending Bushwicks, Ivanhoes and Farmers semipro games. In high school, he was offered Yankees tickets as an incentive to excel in Spanish by a teacher who was an aunt of pitcher Herb Pennock. Shea became proficient en Español and a fixture at the Polo Grounds, where the Yankees still played. Since his mother forbade him to take part in high school football, Shea put his energies into baseball, where he caught and played second base, and into basketball, in which he was a superior player. His school, George Washington High, did not have a basketball team, so Shea and his friends created "Fort Washington Prep," which booked contests against real scholastic squads. Eventually, the scheme was exposed, which did not keep the popular Shea from being elected president of the school's General Organization by the largest margin ever.

The six-foot-tall Shea attended New York University, where he was good enough at football to win a four-year scholarship from Georgetown University; he also played basketball. More importantly, he gained his law degree.

After graduation, his interest in sports continued. He played lacrosse for the Crescent Athletic Club, rated the nation's best. His father-in-law, Thomas Shaw, had been one of biggest bookmakers in New York during the 1920s — a legal activity back then. In the early 1940s Shea operated the Long Island Indians, a farm club of the Washington Redskins football team; he also had a share in an N.F.L. franchise in Boston. His first job after graduation from Law School in 1931 was with the firm of Cullen & Dyckman, where he met George V. McLaughlin, President of the Brooklyn Trust Company, whose patience kept the foundering Dodgers afloat for years. After that Shea worked for the New York State Banking and Insurance Departments and in 1941 became a founding member of the real estate and corporate law firm of Manning, Hollinger & Shea.

By the time Wagner tapped Shea, he was one of the city's most prominent attorneys. Now he was fighting the city's battle in the baseball wars. As an inducement for teams to move, Shea and company could dangle a projected new stadium in Flushing Meadows, Queens — an option O'Malley had rejected.

The quartet approached National League clubs in Cincinnati, Pittsburgh and Philadelphia. The first two expressed some interest, but eventually said no.

Philadelphia wasn't paying any attention to Shea. "In talking to [Bob] Carpenter [of the Phils]," Shea recalled, "I began to realize one thing. This fellow is just like me. He doesn't want to move. Philadelphia is his town and he is going to stay there. He's not going to pick up and leave the place just for money. There are other things which are more important to him. Civic pride? Sure, you can call it that. And when I'm talking to him, I begin to see that I am placing myself in the position of asking him to do the very thing I would never do. Pull out of your own town. That cured me. From then on, I stopped bothering other teams. I was not going to be a party to moving any club, so long as that city had people willing to support it."

The committee, now under Shea's leadership, tried a new tack: expansion.

"At this stage," noted Shea, "my problem is that I am silly enough to think that the National League owed New York something. Here we supported two teams for all those years. Well, the National League didn't feel that way at all. They didn't feel anything. They couldn't have cared less."

So Shea's next gambit was the Continental League.

DAVID PIETRUSZA, *MAJOR LEAGUES*

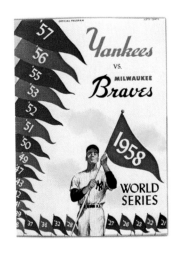

The Yankees avenged their 1957 defeat by defeating Milwaukee in seven games.
Private collection

As Mets manager, Casey's clowning drew attention away from his team's clowning.
Transcendental Graphics

November 16, 1961: The circular Mets logo, designed by sports cartoonist Ray Gatto, was unveiled. It has gone virtually unchanged throughout the history of the club. The shape of the insignia, with its orange stitching, represents a baseball, and the bridge in the foreground symbolizes that the Mets, in bringing back the National League to New York, represent all five boroughs. It's not just a skyline in the background, but has a special meaning. At the left is a church spire, symbolic of Brooklyn, the borough of churches. The second building from the left is the Williamsburg Savings Bank, the tallest building in Brooklyn. Next is the Woolworth Building. After a general skyline view of midtown comes the Empire State Building. At the far right is the United Nations Building. The Mets' colors are Dodger blue and Giant orange, symbolic of the return of National League baseball to New York after the Dodgers and Giants moved to California. Blue and Orange are also the official colors of New York State. NEW YORK METS

Facing page
clockwise from far left:
**Casey's number 37 jersey
is today retired by both
New York clubs; here,
his Mets road jersey.**
Courtesy of Andy Fogel, photograph
by David Arky

**Keith Hernandez made #17
famous at first base in New York,
where only Gil Hodges had
played it as well.**
Courtesy of Andy Fogel, photograph by David Arky

**This ball was signed by every
Brooklyn Dodger who went on to
play for the Mets.**
From the collection of Jerry Stern, photograph by
David Arky

**Willie Mays made the number 24
famous with the New York Giants.
When he returned to the city as a
Met in 1972, he hit a homer in his
first game.**
Courtesy of Andy Fogel, photograph by David Arky

**Signed by the Brooklyn Dodgers,
Roberto Clemente more than anyone
embraced Jackie's legacy.**

Private collection

Most Civil Rights history lessons focus on the holy trinity of Brown, Rosa Parks, and Martin Luther King Jr. — overlooking how Jackie Robinson preceded them all by a decade. Many experts believe that America's tidal wave of change grew from the moment Robinson entered organized baseball. Jimmy Carter once said, "It was sports, racially integrated sports teams, that brought about the change that I think saved the South." Curious about this, I once asked Lou Brock, the Hall of Fame ballplayer whose career began in the still-segregated South, about how baseball's (however tentative) acceptance of black players might have both hastened and facilitated the broader Civil Rights movement that followed. Brock thought for a moment and responded with words I'll never forget. "Baseball," he smiled, "is the background music to America."

(Anyone wanting a fascinating corollary to King's passive-resistance doctrine would be well served by an early conversation between Robinson and Branch Rickey, the cigar-chomping Brooklyn Dodgers boss who needed to confirm that Jackie was the right man to endure the headhunting fastballs, flesh-slicing spikes, and calls of "nigger boy" from opposing dugouts. Robinson asked somewhat testily, "Do you want a player who doesn't have the guts to fight back?" Rickey bellowed, "I'm looking for a ballplayer with the guts not to fight back!")

Dancing down the third-base line menacingly daring to steal home, Robinson eventually slid under America's tag and scored greater respect and appreciation not just for African Americans but, less directly, other excluded groups. His presence allowed the Dodgers a few years later to sign a dark-skinned Puerto Rican named Roberto Clemente, and Clemente's rise to icon status helped beget the rush of Latin Americans into baseball in the 1980s and '90s. (Here, once again, baseball grew up before greater society; it's no surprise that Fernando Valenzuela and Sammy Sosa became megastars before Menudo and Ricky Martin.) The au courant often advocate retiring Clemente's No. 21 throughout baseball, as was done with Robinson's No. 42, but this misses the greater point: Robinson earned that honor not just for opening doors for blacks to play major league ball, but for smacking an entire nation awake.

Speaking of which, it was on the night of April 15, 1997, that Major League Baseball announced — in what then was a stirring surprise — that no big-league ballplayer would ever again be assigned No. 42, that Robinson's jersey would hang retired in every stadium forevermore. All at once, 50,000 fans at Shea Stadium, and millions more watching on television, realized in unison just how vital the memory of Jackie Robinson remains to all of us.

The kids at PS 375 needed no reminder earlier that morning, though. The essays, the march, the class discussions of Jackie Robinson ("Today is just one day," Devine

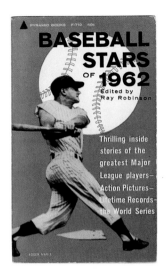

Roger Maris went from hero to villain when he surpassed Ruth's 60-homer mark in 1961. "Baseball Stars of 1962," by Ray Robinson.
Private collection

The 1962 Series rematched the contestants of 1951, the Yanks and Giants—and again after an NL playoff with the Dodgers!
Private collection

**Lighter, front and back: Mr. Met has
been the team's mascot since the beginning, even before Shea Stadium,
which opened in 1964.**

Courtesy of Andy Fogel, photograph by David Arky

Facing page:
**Willie Mays in his prime,
spring training 1956**

Courtesy of Sports Legends and World Heroes,
photograph by Hy Peskin

1969 Mets World Series program

Private collection

Tom Seaver, who came to Shea in 1967, was the Mets first great ballplayer.

Private collection

McRae said, "But it continues") are, at least for me, everlasting reminders of the young teaching the old. Sometimes I wonder where those children are today—where they flew off to, like dandelion spores. I'll probably never know. But I do have an inkling.

When the morning ended, I took one last walk down the halls. Reminders of Jackie Robinson lined them all, pictures and posters and pennants. Watercolor time-lines detailed Robinson's life as both a ballplayer and a man. When I entered the school's main office, another mural was titled, "Branch out towards a Choice Career."

Construction-paper leaves sat on a tree, each with one profession scribbled on it. Doctor. Lawyer. Librarian.

There were 47 different leaves on that tree. Not one of them said "Athlete."

1969 Mets press pin
Courtesy of Andy Fogel, photograph by David Arky

1986 Mets press pin
Courtesy of Andy Fogel, photograph by David Arky

1986 World Series ring
Courtesy of Andy Fogel, photograph by David Arky

Jackie Robinson opened doors in sport and society
for new African American and Hispanic heroes, for both
the Yankees and the Mets.

**Pedro Martinez was already a
likely Hall of Famer when he
signed with the Mets as a free
agent in 2004.**

**The Yankees' Mariano Rivera
may be the greatest relief pitcher
in all of baseball history.**
© New York Yankees

**Carlos Delgado came to
prominence in Toronto and now is
a feared slugger for the Mets.**
© New York Mets

Carlos Beltran patrols
center field for the Mets and
is a five-tool player.

Alex Rodriguez moved from
shortstop to third base when he
joined the Yankees and is an
all-time great.

Willie Randolph, who grew up in
Brooklyn and became a star player
in the Bronx, has established a
new winning tradition as manager
of the Mets.

Just when it seemed the Subway
Series was gone forever, the
2000 fall classic matched the
Mets against the Yankees.

The New York Times/Redux,
photograph by Barton Silverman

Acknowledgments

Many hands make light the work, it is said. And while it is troubling to think of how much harder we might have had to work to produce this book, we certainly have a legion of people to thank, from artifact donors and essayists to designers and archivists, from design and production wizards to proofers and copyeditors. But as with any list a handful of individuals lay claim to our deepest gratitude, for their roles in the Glory Days exhibit and particularly this companion book.

Susan Henshaw Jones and Sarah Henry have been foursquare behind the concept from the moment Larry Simon proposed it to the Museum of the City of New York. Their unswerving support has permitted the curator, Ann Meyerson, and her consultant, yours truly, to regard the inevitable calamities that face every exhibition in progress as mere bumps in the road.

Joe Tessitore and Phil Friedman of Collins have been wonderfully cooperative and understanding. More than just publishers, they became friends of the project and the museum, although in the rush to ready this book for printing we surely stretched the bounds of their goodwill.

The concept and structure of the exhibition were Ann Meyerson's idea and I am enduringly grateful for her invitation to serve as her curatorial sidekick. She has been of vital help to the book, cajoling collectors, gathering primary historical materials, and overseeing photo shoots. Invaluable to both of us across the board has been the museum's Susan Gail Johnson, whose role on the book expanded as deadlines neared and need arose; she more than earned her spurs as the book's managing editor.

Michael Gericke and Don Bilodeau, as well as the whole Pentagram Design team, brilliantly conceived a platform for the exhibit that would fit the book too. Urshula Barbour and Paul Carlos of Pure+Applied supplied additional layers of visual appeal that make this a baseball-history book and exhibition companion like no other. Isaac Gertman of P+A was a valued member of the design and production group too.

As Casey Stengel used to say when complimented on his success with the Yankees, "I couldn'ta done it without my players." Us neither. And our players comprise four distinct but equally indispensable squads: the lenders, almost incredibly committed to helping the museum; the archivists, who went the extra furlong with hurried deliveries, even last minute electronic file transfers; freelance experts in words and pictures whom we subjugated to no less arduous schedules; and the unfailingly responsive museum personnel, each of them performing a role without which the entire effort might have failed.

First among the lenders is Stephen Wong, who not only photographed much of his own fabulous collection for the book but also introduced to us his network of expert memorabilia hunters. Bruce Dorskind and Jerry Stern are two names you'll find attached to scores of items in the book; their passion for the game and the era glow from the photographs they shared with us. Also extending themselves on our account—including in some cases to the extent of permitting or creating photo shoots in their homes—were, in no particular order: Millie and Bill Gladstone, Hank Seiden, Brian Strum, Bill Horowitz, Peter Knobler, Mike Santo, Angela Sarro, Kevin Bean, Ron Leff, Mark Cooper, Bernie Hubert, Stephen Schlein, Andy Fogel, Jerry Liebowitz, E. Lisk Wyckoff, the unfailingly helpful Gary Cypres, the incomparable artist of the glory days Andy Jurinko, and two different gentlemen who share the same name and kind spirit: Bob Mayer (one of them is married to Adelyn; gentlemen, you know which one you are). Kudos also to Peter Brown, Jack McCormack, and Phil Wood. The Yankees and the Mets were gracious and responsive, particularly Debbie Tymon of the former and Jill Grabill of the latter. Elizabeth Lombardi and Anna Isaacson of the Brooklyn Cyclones were great, too.

Working with the photo archivists and the family members of the era's great lensmen was a joy. Bonnie Crosby shared with us some of the evocative photos that her father, Barney Stein, shot of the Brooklyn Dodgers. Adriana Reynolds made it possible for us to include some unpublished or long unseen work by her late husband, Brian Reynolds, known to sport historians by his original name—the great Hy Peskin. Jim O'Leary and Greg Oliver of Sport Media Group rummaged through thousands of images from the dear departed SPORT magazine to unearth some gems for us. Mark Rucker of Transcendental Graphics, with whom the editor has worked for decades, was as helpful and inventive as ever. Longtime colleague Pat Kelly of the National Baseball Hall of Fame Library was aided this time around by Andrew Newman. Marilyn Pettit of the Brooklyn Historical Society made our impossible requests seem routine. Michael Massmann of Redux helped us nab a great *New York Times* image of the Subway Series of 2000. And Claus Guglberger, photo archivist of the *New York Daily News*, was vital to the original concept of the exhibit.

Among the wordsmiths, first among equals is Harvey Frommer, a consultant to the exhibit from its earliest days and, with his wife Myrna Katz Frommer, a great expert on all things baseball and New York (and that city within a city, Brooklyn). Bob

Gruber and Bob McGee had stories galore that enriched our understanding. As to our esteemed essayists, we'll let their own words commend themselves to you. David Pietrusza's last-minute contributions were small but choice (or as Brooklynites once described Dodger Dixie Walker, cherce). Jed Thorn supplied the copyediting. Donna Habersaat aided in image roundup. Erica Freudenberger and several unnamed but hawkeyed readers shared the proofreading burden.

Among the pictosmiths, if there is such a word, David Arky earned his laurel by creating a great volume of object photographs under trying circumstances with surpassing skill and unfailing good humor. And if there is an image doctor corresponding to Neil Simon's storied role as play doctor, Ken Allen is it, working his magic to make neglected monochrome negatives yield their secrets and decaying color work spring back into bloom.

Last and thus occupying a position of high honor are the exceptional museum personnel whom we thank here inadequately but with full hearts: Melanie Bower, Eddie Jose Bartolomei, Liora Cobin, Barbara Elam, Ann Go, Abby Lepold, Karen Murphy, Autumn Nyiri, George O'Dell, Julia Van Haaften, Deborah Dependahl Waters, Sloane Whidden, and Shelley Wilson.

J.T.
Editor

Credits

Images credited to Stephen Wong are from The Stephen Wong Collection.

Images by Hy Peskin appear courtesy of Sports Legends and World Heroes.

Images credited as Courtesy of the Barney Stein Collection LLC are copyrighted by the LLC and Barney Stein.

Images credited to the SPORT Collection: Photographs courtesy of The *SPORT* Collection, ©SPORT Gallery Inc.

Andy Jurinko painting appears courtesy of the artist.

Courtesy of the authors, passages appear from *It Happened in Brooklyn: An Oral History of Growing Up in the Borough in the 1940s, 1950s, and 1960s* (Harcourt, 1993), ©Harvey and Myrna Katz Frommer; and *It Happened In Manhattan: An Oral History of Life in the City During the Mid-20th Century* (Berkley, 2001), ©Harvey and Myrna Katz Frommer.

Excerpt from *Major Leagues: The Formation, Sometimes Absorption and Mostly Inevitable Demise of 18 Professional Baseball Organizations, 1871 to Present.* McFarland and Company, 1991. ©1991 David Pietrusza.

Passages from *The Greatest Ballpark Ever: Ebbets Field and the Story of the Brooklyn Dodgers* (Rutgers, 2005; ©Bob McGee 2005) appear courtesy of Bob McGee.

Images of *Baseball Register* covers appear courtesy of The Sporting News.

PHOTOGRAPHS PAGES 1–8:
1. Ball caught and kept by a young Dodger fan. Courtesy of Stephen Schlein
2-3. Mantle and Stengel in the dugout, May 1953 Museum of the City of New York, LOOK Collection, photograph by Robert Lerner
4-5. Babe Ruth's bat Courtesy of E. Lisk Wyckoff, photograph by David Arky
6-7. Heaven comes to Brooklyn Courtesy of the Brooklyn Public Library, Brooklyn Collection
8. Don Newcombe, February 1951 Museum of the City of New York, LOOK Collection, photograph by Frank Bauman